THE
PROMISED
LAND

THE

And Othe

PROMISED LAND
Courthouse Adventures

WEYMAN I. LUNDQUIST

Illustrations by Joan Hanley

SECTION OF LITIGATION
AMERICAN BAR ASSOCIATION

The views herein expressed by the author do not
necessarily represent the American Bar Association
or the Section of Litigation.

American Bar Association, Chicago 60611
Produced by the ABA Press

Library of Congress Catalog Card Number 70688
ISBN 0-89707-300-2

Cover design and illustrations by Joan Hanley.

*To trial lawyers, my
lifelong adversaries
and friends*

Contents

Illustrations

THE
PROMISED
LAND

Once
in a Month of
Sundays

During his first jury trial, a young partner of mine told me of his concern that "nowadays, only once in a month of Sundays does a lawyer get to try a case, particularly a jury case." That comment made me reflect on my own good fortune in frequently trying cases and having for three decades watched other warriors of the courtroom at work from Boston, Massachusetts, to Nome, Alaska.

The human drama of a jury trial involves the soul of American life. The exquisite wisdom of the jury process is that ordinary citizens are involved in determining what law is and will be. What makes this trial arena so compelling? The answer: It represents the quintessence of what is right about America. David can take on Goliath. Change can occur. Injury can have its just redress.

These stories, then, arise from over a quarter century of trial adventures from Nome on the Bering Sea where Russia begins, to Boston, around which (as the locals would have it) the world revolves, to San Francisco, which is "out west" to Bostonians, "outside" to Alaskans, but "The City" to those who reside there.

From my adventures I have a treasury of lawyers' war stories, mostly fancy, and even then embellished to come out as I want them to.

In the made-up stories, real names are used on occasion. When this is done, as with my references to Robert Bowditch, Justice Boochever, and Dick Guggenhime, the event is based on fact in a story otherwise made up. Elsewhere, characters, incidents, and dialogue imagine people, trials, and court-related adventures as I sense they would have occurred. In fiction, as in life, the trial courtroom holds adventure.

Let me begin with a favorite story.

The
Promised
Land

THE COMPLAINANT

Thumper Johnson was a one-legged trapper and the sometimes captain of his own ship, the *Queen of Sheba*, which served Lake Louise (about 150 miles northeast of Anchorage, Alaska, and 30 miles west of the old Fairbanks highway). The Thumper moniker came from his having a wooden leg that thumped about on the old Queen, and the sometimes-ship-captain reputation developed because Thumper sailed only when he wanted. His was the only sizable boat on the lake, and Thumper was needed by the hardy souls who nestled in the wilds around Lake Louise to trap, hunt, fish, or maybe even prospect.

Now, Alaska had its share of characters in 1959, but Thumper was in the certified class. He was the genuine article. His physique was a living caricature of Popeye the Sailor. He had a massive upper body, with a scruffy halo of graying hair encircling a bald head. Unlike Popeye, however, his dress was basic bush: heavy wool pants and a plaid wool shirt, connected by orange suspenders. He wore one boot and hobbled with his wooden thumper, affixing a snowshoe to it in winter. Snow-shoed, he could move almost as fast as the rabbits he seemed to catch in abundance. As Thumper was described by old Doc Pierce, the Copper River bush pilot: "He is your typical poor quality fur trapper." Not that the rabbit furs Thumper took were poor: They were damn good. It's just that good-quality fur animals—mink, marten, wolverine, fox—avoided Thumper's traps. They probably didn't care for the smell.

Thumper had a misty past. He didn't open up much about it. Bush etiquette being what it is, people didn't inquire. Thumper had been on the lake longer than anyone else. He was, in fact, the only year-round resident. Living there was not easy, but it sure agreed with Thumper, and for some years it had seemed to agree with his wife, Shirley. Shirley's disappearance was one of many mysteries in Thumper's past.

Maybe there was some tension in their relationship and just no Dear Abby to write to or parson to talk with. One spring, Shirley just wasn't there. Thumper had a persuasive story about her heading out just before freeze-up for a trip to the Wasilla dentist to deal with a tough toothache problem. She took their motor skiff to get to the highway end of the lake. There she had planned on a hitch with Doc Pierce, who was hauling caribou killers in and out of a local airstrip. A storm came up after Shirley went out, and "that," as Thumper put it, "was it for old Shirley." The only thing found was a wrecked skiff. The story was hard to touch, according to the marshal. Anyway, no one believed that Thumper would give up his skiff and motor even if he could give up Shirley at the same time. The story held.

What started the mysterious disappearance story wasn't all that unusual in the bush. Engineer Tom Square, who was an Alaska Railroad train driver, and Thumper went on a several-day toot that took them from Lake Louise a hundred miles to the one close bar, then back to Doc Pierce's Quonset at the end of the lake. Doc wasn't there, but using his Quonset was quite all right with Doc, just as long as they would restock it. That was expected bush etiquette. Thumper and

Tom got to about a two- or three-bottle day—then Tom's memory gets fuzzy. He thinks that Thumper tells him something about Shirley being done in, or drowned, and Thumper isn't too sad. But he told Tom—he *maybe* told Tom, to be more accurate—that he knew that if there were no corpse, there could be no question of foul play. Because it was an unusually hard winter and Shirley was all froze up, he just made a big stew, and that was that.

Now, that's a story to raise some eyebrows, but it does tell you about Thumper. Thumper is a survivor. Oh, yes: Tom also remembers visiting Thumper the winter Shirley left. He swears there was always a big stewpot on the stove. Well, so much for the mystery of Shirley's demise. Nothing ever came of it, but "maybe," said Norm Filer, the high court clerk, "maybe it made Thumper more law-abiding." And maybe that's why he did the complaining about the Point Wrangell Baptists.

For sure, it was Thumper who started the whole business that brought the Wrangell Baptist pack to trial. On one of his excursions around Lake Louise, he was surprised (and it's safe to say, irritated) to discover thirty-seven Baptists on a large spit of land, which he avowed was located in *his* best fur territory. Thumper had caught a few otters there once. To aggravate the intrusion on his public land, they even had their own boat and had shown no interest in making any transport use of the *Queen of Sheba*. In fact, the size of their boat, bought from proceeds of the good Reverend Doheney's earlier professional activities, made it look as if Captain Thumper Johnson and his *Queen* might see competition on Lake Louise. Individualist, entrepreneur, and capitalist that he was, Thumper became downright articulate about what a businessman does *not* need: "competition—from Baptists!"

So, Thumper made the arduous journey to Anchorage and harangued the marshal, who wasn't much interested because "if I had to start to relocate settlers from Alaska public lands, I'd need the army and the air force. With Lake Louise included, the navy, too, for half the damn citizens—the crazy, wild half—is settled on public land privately."

The marshal's answers didn't sit well with Thumper. No Baptists were going to take over *his* public land. Snooping around to find out who might really care, Thumper didn't have any trouble discovering that the Bureau of Indian Affairs people viewed the land as theirs. Thumper contacted them.

The BIA is an agency distinguished by its lack of talent. It does, however, have geniuses: geniuses at doing the wrong thing, the wrong way. Consider that its bureaucrats are essentially trustees and managers for all the Indians and Indian nations of this country. Try to put aside the fact that they don't like Indians and generally don't know how to manage anything, and focus on how they routinely operate. They can't keep the records for the funds they get. Then they claim that what they do get they don't need to invest to earn for the beneficiaries. If they do invest, they accept interest at 4 percent. Their fiscal expertise is displayed in approving their own expense accounts and preparing bigger budgets for next year's misfeasances. Misfeasance is their basic product. Malfeasance enters the picture when they think real hard. Even though they don't often think, the agency is always in trouble. "And unlike other government agencies, they work hard first to accomplish, then to defend their screwing up," as Norm Filer reported.

So Thumper Johnson contacted Horace Fiddle, the local BIA headman, pointing out to him that the BIA had land in the Lake Louise area and there were squatters on that land. What made it even worse, according to information sieved out of the BIA secretarial pool: some of the squatters might be Indians. Indians settling on their own land without BIA authority committed a worse offense than if done by your basic white. Fiddle was ready to call in the cavalry.

Thumper probably didn't have to lay it on much to say the Wrangell Point Baptists claimed Indian status. The Reverend called them all Native Sons of God. This, of course, aroused

Fiddle and the BIA even more, for if there were native sons of anything out there in the great U.S. of A., they had an obligation to do native-son things the BIA law-decreed way. For instance, Indians were required to form tribes so the BIA could administer them. Using native lands without BIA approval and taking property management into their own hands was an attack on the fundamental BIA way of life. As the D.C. bigwigs assessed it, if it started in Alaska, it could spread elsewhere. Some natives might not need the BIA. They might do their own thing. And if people started properly managing the land they used, the whole bureau was in jeopardy. The BIA sprang into action.

Had General Custer been alive, the BIA would have selected him to handle the matter. Fortunately, there was no cavalry in Alaska. Marshal Coleburn knew far too much about Alaska, law, and justice to risk his neck. As he told the BIA's Fiddle, "If it were robbery or murder, even rape, we'd help out, but something as serious as this . . . invasion, I call it . . . invasion of U.S. land. This is a matter of Executive Responsibility; maybe it's an act of war. It's just too damned much for the U.S. marshal's office."

Well, how far Fiddle tried to run with that, we don't know. President Nixon never mentioned it and, so far as the locals knew, even the two Alaska senators and the lone representative did a duck. But the BIA wouldn't be stopped. Suit must be brought.

The BIA had achieved dubious fame in Alaska long before statehood in 1959. The bureau had managed to disrupt Eskimo culture by imposing the "American Way" in hamlets on the northern coast of Alaska and in larger settlements such as Nome and Kotzebue. It did this by taking children from their ancestral homes to schools hundreds, even thousands of miles away, where they were taught things of no useful application in their villages. When they returned home, there was no "American Way" to live. Painful schisms developed between old and young. The only American "value" that reached the natives was beer or whiskey, which didn't do the Eskimos a whole lot of good. The one positive effect this cultural devastation produced (if anything the BIA does can be called positive) was to make all the other Alaskans more interested and concerned for the Eskimos than they otherwise might have been. In doing its deeds, the BIA spent about half the federal money that trickled into Alaska—at great harm to everyone. In federal fashion, the bureau used each year's screwups to justify more money for the next year's budget. Left to its own devices, the BIA would have had a substantial edge on the Defense Department in running up the federal deficit.

As the assistant United States attorney in Alaska usually burdened with trying to defend government screwups, such as condemning land for access roads to highways that didn't exist, or prosecuting public benefactors (like U.S. Army Sergeant Rodkins, who had given away a record amount of government supplies to nice people, albeit most of them his relatives), I had expected to draw this Wrangell duty. I was relieved when I found out I would not have to try the case. The BIA was sending out its own lawyer from Washington (the D.C. Washington) to defend the sanctity of BIA lands from the intrusions of a small group of settlers who had earmarked the lands for religious purposes—a colony of Baptists, "put in place by God."

It was a comfort for me not to have to tangle with a suit that Judge Hodge deemed an "inanity" in a conversation he did not have with me about the case. I know he did not have it, because even as Judge Hodge told me his views of the case, he said, "This is a conversation you are not having with me." And though I was young and zealous in upholding the law, I also knew right from wrong and the power of federal district judges. It was right that a judge not talk about pending cases. Judge Hodge was a righteous judge.

With some theoretical sense, then, of where the judge might be coming from on this case, I held the personal view that either the BIA attorney (who could have fobbed the case

off on me to try) or his "Butt-In Agency" client deserved
high marks either for stupidity or blind courage in wanting
to go it alone with this trial before Judge Hodge. At the time,
I had no idea that half the senior BIA lawyers in D.C. were
ready to make this case their cause célèbre. This would be
the first big BIA trial in Alaska since it became a state. By
1961, the feds felt Alaska was entitled to a statehood showing
of BIA justice.

I did all I could to encourage the BIA lawyers by pointing
out the judge's obvious antipathy toward me, his esteem for
legal scholars, and the fact that there were none in Alaska,
according to the selfsame judge. I pointed out that lawyers
coming from D.C. had at least a chance to satisfy the judge's
intellectual yearnings. To assure smooth sailing by the BIA
lawyers, I promised them I'd keep the United States attorney
awake and sober enough to move their *pro hac vice* admission—no small task. This would further ensure that the judge
would know how important the case was and not stigmatize
it as a petty matter in which a mere assistant United States
attorney was being allowed to argue for admitting non-
Alaskans to practice in order to handle it.

My own views of the ill wisdom of this bureaucratic adventure were the kindest held by any person associated with
the federal court in Anchorage. Marshal Coleburn—who had
an honest, admired, and self-avowed reputation for being
willing to "dash in where fools feared to tread" because "if
I won't do it, how can I ask my men to?"—refused to get
involved. In fact, he assigned Hans Larson, his dumbest
deputy, to assist the BIA in serving papers in the case. Larson
did not make too impressive a start, because he got lost
somewhere north of Anchorage while trying to serve the
complaints on the defendants. The marshal refused to send
anyone to look for him, telling Russell Trent, the local United
States attorney, that Hans had the marshal's manual and a
Coast and Geodetic Survey map, so he was as well equipped
as anyone to find the defendants, and himself. The marshal

was confident of Hans's return in any event, for coming up was a three-day-weekend Labor Day Matanuska Fair holiday. Barring his demise, Hans would not miss that.

Norman Filer, the chief clerk for all the Alaska federal courts, civil and criminal, was a taciturn man with a large responsibility. No federal district was as large, had as few people, or maintained as many courthouses per capita (although sometimes located more than a thousand miles apart). When Filer spoke, he was not given to fancy words, although he knew ones just as good as Judge Hodge's, such as "inane" and "farcical." If he were to go low brow, Norman would stoop to phrases like "dumb" or "stupid." When he called this the "goddamndest ignoramus lawsuit" he'd seen since they arrested Chinamen in Nome for smoking opium in their own temple, you knew it was not a well-considered piece of litigation, at least in Alaskan terms.

THOSE COMPLAINED AGAINST

With this little prelude, I should get down to the details, and maybe even some of the facts that led up to *BIA v. The Wrangell Point Christian Baptist Colony, Reverend Francis Doheney, and DOES 1 through 100.* From the days when western New York State was "the frontier," fervent groups in search of "promised land" have headed westward. As a consequence, there are those who would hold for California as the kook, cult, commune, religious-fanatic mecca of the United States. But as Marshal Coleburn said, "If West and wilderness are magnets for the crazies, the best ones will get to Alaska: Alaska is the most westward place, has the most wilderness. It gets the very cream of the religious perverts and willy-wackies." As the marshal explained, "It's not just that their ideas are wilder. They are also deeper entrenched, and the believers are strong, tough survivors to get here. They aren't bad people like some dopehead—and a dopehead can come down or get cold or strung out, but not your basic Alaska religious freak. He believes what he believes and that's it, come hell or high water, or the U.S. Constitution."

The origins of the Wrangell Point Baptists deserve noting. A few of the seniors were Polish types who came to Alaska when Franklin Delano Roosevelt opened the Matanuska Valley for farming in the thirties. They were invariably tough. Raising anything in Alaska is tough, but thirty years of farming voluntarily in Alaska is like enjoying a hard labor sentence. Although the Matanuska seniors were past their physical prime, when it came to mental rigidity they were never stronger. When they dug into a position, they'd hang to it like a tick or a leech. They just didn't know about letting go of anything, least of all their views. They weren't leaders, but they sure were staunch followers: the kind that, if the leader slows down, will march right on over him to the front. This group joined up with the Reverend's pack after the latter reached Alaska.

The Wrangell Point Baptists' chief was the Reverend Francis Doheney, and that man was a leader. He was Protestant Irish, for starters. Somewhere along the way he'd gotten into a Baptist theology school in Oklahoma for his degree in the Reverend profession. Before he settled into leading a religious pack (the Wrangell Point Baptists didn't go for flocks or for shepherds; they wanted a pack leader), he had done a residency as a California real estate salesman.

Now, I know from personal experience that there is no more religious, fervent, or patriotic group than those who hustled land sales in California in the late fifties and early sixties. It bordered on apotheosis for them to convince their customers to buy a lot, or a lot of lots. As the salesmen said to their customers, "Land would make 'them' wealthy," with typical sales ambiguity as to the "them" involved. "It was the key to every great fortune." "This parcel is unique" (some of it sure as hell was, with no roads or water to serve it) "and limited in supply." "People like Ben Franklin and other patriots had extolled owning it." On top of all that, the commissions were damn good. Well, the Reverend had eased up to his preaching by selling land, to the point where he managed and inspired, or maybe inspired and managed, dozens of salesmen. Doheney had made a lot of money.

His California success became so renowned that at some point Doheney got into a scrape with the California Department of Real Estate. Somehow, the Reverend was involved with the placement of water pumps that caused lots to front on brooks or streams in the dry season (or at least in the selling season part of the dry season)—and for sure on weekends, when loads of customers were delivered C.O.D. to his salesmen. The Reverend felt it was necessary for potential owners to get the feel of the two rainy months when water flowed, even if they bought in the summer. As he pointed out to the Department of Real Estate, the sales literature made no warranties that the streams were permanent or that they flowed regularly. Inasmuch as the waterfront lots sold for thousands more, the DRE had the feeling that the customers paying the big price assumed there was more water available than during the two months of winter and the pump-watered weekends. The department started to shut the Reverend down, talking of maybe fining him and maybe even prosecuting him for fraud.

The Reverend didn't want to waste his energies on the mundane technicalities of commercial real-estate law. Rather than enlighten the California real estate people, he invested some of his hard-earned, God-blessed commissions in a bus and headed for Alaska, where he would continue to be guided by God.

The Reverend reveled in a crowd. During his land-sales days, many times he had arranged for a busload of Los Angeles or San Francisco blue-collars to trek up to some godforsaken but outstanding land subdivision. He had a reputation for being able to convert 100 percent of them into owners of second home lots in inaccessible areas of the state. This was more remarkable than you'd think, for many of them could not even afford first homes. Prudence on the Reverend's part required his commissions to come from the down payments. Since that was often the only payment, the Reverend had sold many lots a number of times. Indeed, legend had it that in one six-month period he had sold or supervised others who sold 327 lots in a 200-lot desert city somewhere between L.A. and Las Vegas.

With his affection for a crowd and an empty bus to fill, it was natural that he met up with a group of unhappy Detroit-area Baptist farmers in Seattle on their way to Alaska. The farmers had been disenfranchised by the post-World War II real estate and the industrial age. They had their own land troubles because they had sold their small midwestern farms to developer-speculators who proceeded to make a fortune from them! With what few remaining funds they had, they were heading to Alaska to start again the hard life that nurtured them. Reverend Doheney knew about people with land problems. Because of his own Christian involvement and profit from land, there was a natural affinity between Doheney and these Baptists. The fact that there were more young women than men in the group probably didn't hurt, either. Ten days later at Dawson Creek in British Columbia, they elected him group leader. By the time they arrived at Tok Junction in Alaska, the Reverend was retained as their pastor.

The thirty-one midwestern Detroit Baptists plus six old Polish "Baptists" from the Matanuska settled on Wrangell Point in Lake Louise. The Matanuska Poles were cousins to some of the midwestern Baptists and, despite nearly thirty years of farming in central Alaska, wanted more challenges before they packed it in or up. Precisely where God joined the two groups has always been a little unclear, but all agreed that God had to be involved to make an old Matanuska farmer look for a wilderness challenge.

THE ACTION BEGINS

It was no big deal for folks to go and settle throughout Alaska in the sixties. Indeed, the Feds had a special homesteading program to encourage it. Many people played at homesteading to get their land. I say "played," for to "prove up a homestead" one had to reside on and farm a section. Now, in Alaska, to farm most places was a laugh, the climate being inimical even to weeds. To "reside" and to "farm" therefore took a wealthy person with a sound grubstake. Still, with a little imaginative description of a radish crop and a tent, many found themselves able to acquire legal homestead title. Needless to say, the local judiciary was aware of the practice, because the final step in granting the homestead involved a court proceeding.

The easiest and most valuable homestead land to procure was near cities and lawyers. The homesteader could have a steady job to support the farm. The lawyer could write the legal necessities. Naturally, the land close to cities was homesteaded up. So, as Marshal Coleburn said, "The whole damn state is pocketed here and there with squatters and settlers in, and who the hell knows or cares? They've only done what the city-dwelling homesteaders do, except the bush people make it work and work at it." You have to appreciate that with fewer than three hundred thousand people then and an area that would stretch over most of the lower forty-eight states if placed atop them, a few folks living here and there did not rise to federal-problem status in the marshal's eyes. In fact, meeting people in the wilds once in a while could be a nice change from encountering a moose or a grizzly. So the marshall asked, "Who cares where the Wrangell Point Baptists settle?" Well, the BIA did, that's who. Thumper Johnson had spilled the beans about the Baptists, so the BIA swung into action. As Norman Filer reported: "Since they have historically screwed the Indians and Eskimos out of land that was rightfully theirs, they are scrupulous about protecting it for their agency in accordance with Principle and Policy."

Into Judge H. Waterloo Hodge's court the BIA charged with evictions and injunctions and trespasses and ejectments. Fifty-seven pages' worth in the first complaint. "First Complaint," it said right on it. Judge Hodge muttered, "Fifty-seven pages, and that's only the First Complaint. What else can there be? I've already read seven pages, and I've found thirteen new words." I should explain that the judge was in my office a lot. He didn't like to sully his own—"not judicial," he said—but he did use mine to store things: milk and sandwiches on the windowsill, fish in season, heavy winter gear, old books (not usually legal). We never discussed pending cases, only personal matters—his "views" on pending cases.

Hodge was the first and only Nome homegrown boy to leave, then return after getting out of law school. Most of Alaska's lawyers had come to the state after practicing outside. They lacked the instincts Hodge grew up with, which gave Hodge's law an indigenous quality. And his quick, terse way with words as a lawyer made him an obvious and popular choice as territorial judge. Following statehood in 1959, Senator Gruening made certain that Hodge became Alaska's first federal district judge. In this high and lifetime office, the slight, bespectacled judge grew to be commensurate in popular respect to Alaska's own size. Unlike many judges who are often wrong but never in doubt, Hodge was often in doubt, but when he figured things out he was seldom wrong. He was not, however, loaded up with patience. Shilly-shallying courtroom lawyers or circumlocutory writing ticked the hell out of him. Reading the First Complaint, he said he wasn't smart enough to solve a book of problems: "A page at a time is more my style."

That complaint provided the best legal strategy the Wrangell Point people had. They started out intending to defend themselves with God's help. A fifty-seven-page First Complaint gave them a lot to defend. What they couldn't know, not being experts in Judge Hodge's court, was that they really needed to defend seven pages—that's all the judge would read. On occasion he did get up to twelve, but it had to be an "unusually interesting brief." This was "only a goddamn complaint."

Someone in the Wrangell group—probably the Reverend himself, for he had a decent exposure to law through its pursuit of him—figured a simple "we didn't do it" and "if we did, God told us to" reply would be the right approach. Unfortunately, God was slow in inspiring the group to put its ideas on paper, and no answer to the governments case got filed.

With no answer on file, the BIA, seemingly more interested in screwing up its case than winning, filed a Motion for Default Judgment. A default judgment is a sharp lawyer's way of trying to win for a client before the other side gets a chance in court. The BIA motion was even longer than the First Complaint. In fact, everything the bureau filed was longer than the First Complaint, because a copy of the First Complaint was always attached as an exhibit. Judge Hodge, a friend of the forest, viewed these paper-mountain motions as a direct attack on Alaska's timber reserves. He was especially sensitive about this because of his upbringing above the Arctic Circle, where an eighteen inch tree will have taken two hundred years to grow.

The BIA procedural approach raised the judge's temperature to unprecedented heights. Instead of providing a pleading of several pages (three was what the judge really liked, with a beginning, a middle, and a conclusion) to acquaint him with the case, the BIA filed its fifty-seven-page "book." Without giving the other side a fair chance to read it, the bureau filed a motion to default the defendants when an answer was only a month overdue. Judge Hodge's unpublished rule concerning defaults was that a pleading filed "sixty days after a due date is timely, usually." He might allow more time when the parties were far apart. "Far apart" was to be understood literally or figuratively. People lived far apart in Alaska, and travel was hard, so it was challenging to get papers around. Figurative distance existed when the litigious positions of the parties were 180 degrees apart. The judge told me, "A little judicial delay can be a good way of making people resolve their problems themselves, if they need to bad enough."

In the BIA-Wrangell case sixty days after the filing, Judge Hodge was only up to page 7 of the First Complaint, so allowing the Wrangell Point Baptists a few months to think about their answer was to him only common sense. This was particularly true because the BIA, with umpteen lawyers and months to work on the complaint, had written one that set forth alternative causes of action. One of the judge's unwritten rules was that alternative causes of action were disfavored. Alternative causes of action are a sort of "if we don't win this way, we win that way" approach. In Hodge's view, if a party didn't know what he, she, or it wanted for justice, how could the judge, much less the opposition? Finally, attaching an exhibit of pleadings that were already on file was, in the judge's eye, like bringing ice to Nome in January. "What's there is there" was his oft-expressed view. If he wouldn't read it the first time, he wasn't going to go for some attached exhibit to fool him into reading it. The BIA lawyers tried to convince the filing clerk that including the First Complaint made studying their motions easier for the judge. "Only heavier" was the good clerk's reply.

If the Wrangell Point people had hired a competent local practitioner like John Manders or Bailey Sanders from the outset, they might have won going away. Certainly the case would not have come to trial when it did—in less than two years. Heavy betting in the Murmac Saloon (advertised in Anchorage as "The Bar Where the Bar meets") was that with good lawyers the trial could be avoided at least until Judge Hodge retired (eight or ten years thence). In fact, John Manders and Bailey Sanders—the two senior members of the Murmac Bar Association, having been lawyers in Alaska for eighteen and fifteen years respectively—had active practices, yet only in extreme circumstances did they ever try a case. To be sure, each of them had a lot of cases "going." For Manders and Sanders, "going" meant that bills still went out on occasion for the cases acquired in their early years of practice. Manders explained to young lawyers that this approach to billing was wholly appropriate, since he thought a great deal about those cases. John Manders was by stateside standards probably the most respected lawyer in Alaska. He had come to Alaska from San Francisco in his mid-forties, and he looked more like a San Francisco judge than an Alaska lawyer. He talked like a San Franciscan, eschewing the first person. His clothes were fashioned after the style of the great Solicitor General John William Davis who had so many United States Supreme Court victories. While John's record for action wasn't great, not getting to trial meant he didn't have many losses.

In a Murmac Bar Association panel discussion of the case, Manders explained to the younger barristers attending that "one should start with a simple Motion for a Continuance to Respond, Pending Evaluation of the Complaint." Such motions were OK with Judge Hodge, and John reasoned that the judge probably would not "fully evaluate the complaint for at least several years," so he wouldn't push the Wrangell folks to make such a procedural evaluation themselves absent gold's being found on the land.

Bailey Sanders, despite his Kansas populist upbringing, favored a more sophisticated approach. He wanted to "Move to Change the Venue to Nome." His reasoning was that the most crowded court calendar was in Anchorage. A venue change would give the Nome court more use. This would be efficient for the entire federal court system in Alaska. It would justify the federal funds used to keep the Nome courthouse open, and it would be good for the local economy. He also offered the view that Anchorage jurors were more prejudiced against the BIA than those in Nome. There were more BIA people to know in Anchorage. As attorney for the Wrangell pack, he'd argue that even the BIA was entitled to a fair trial. Hodge liked that sort of legal genius.

The consensus was that either motion would chew up several years. Regarding the congested calendar aspect of the motion, its weakness was that this was a judge trial. Hodge, being the only federal judge in the District of Alaska, would try it whether in Nome or Anchorage, and so far as we lawyers knew, the judge seemed to pack his prejudices with him wherever he traveled. The judge might evince concern that his Anchorage caseload was heavy, while his Nome load was light, and he did like to get to Nome on occasion— especially if it would be good for the local economy.

This was good theoretical lawyering; it wasn't necessary. Indeed, as Joe Slade, the Murmac bartender, observed, "Most times, just leaving things alone works out better than what the best lawyers can do." While that wasn't a popular sentiment with the Murmac bar, in the case of the hearing on the default motion, it sure was right.

The BIA was all geared up for this hearing, wanting a first round knockout. The papers were well done, "no typos at all and damn little erasing," the judge's venerable in-court law clerk reported. No opposition to the default had been filed. Fiddle for the BIA, having ascertained this by examining the docket as recently as seventy-two hours before the hearing, called back the information to his legal chiefs in D.C. Assured of no opposition, a three-lawyer BIA team took off to argue an unopposed motion. They were joined by the regional BIA counsel from Portland, Oregon. The latter was less enthusiastic about the trip than his D.C. confreres. He had been in court in Alaska before. For the three from Washington, Messrs. Rodgers, Feldstein, and Straub, it was a different story. This was their first Alaska boondoggle, and they wanted to make the most of it.

Marshal Coleburn in those days served as a personification of what would later be the Freedom of Information Act. He believed public records were just that, except sometimes in criminal cases. Coleburn reported that the BIA expense vouchers filed through his office indicated that "a team of three lawyers is necessary because we want to make certain of an early, dispositive victory against this invasion of BIA lands." Coleburn's personal view was that "while they've come loaded for bear, they are more likely to be shot than to shoot." The marshal had prophecy.

Coleburn, born in San Diego, California, had been sent by the Army to Alaska in World War II. He had managed to visit every bleak outpost in Attu, Barrow, and even out by Siberia and into the Brooks Range for cold-weather survival training. The army with its typical idiosyncratic logic, had sent a lot of Southern Californians to those places. Clement Coleburn was the only one for whom the training took. Out of the army, he did a little GI Bill time studying sociology or some related humanities science. By '47 he was back in Alaska as a deputy territorial officer. He loved Alaska, only going "outside" if he had to, and this usually involved transporting the meanest of criminals out of Alaska. "Taking them home," Clement called it.

Coleburn, though small, carried a big pistol. No one had ever known him to use it. He was single-handedly responsible for the geographically largest marshal's office in the United States. Considering its populace—Native Americans, Indian and Eskimo; Military families; adventurers; fishermen; hunters; and God's Chosen, not to mention the "city folks" in Anchorage, Juneau, and Fairbanks, in that order—it presented marvelously diverse problems. Somehow this dour Scotchman with a soft word and a rare smile could subdue almost any volatile situation. If there was one thing Marshal Coleburn knew, it was that in Alaska you can "never go by the book." That wisdom had earned him great respect for being able to get things done, although it was best not to inquire just how he did it. Judge Hodge was in charge of deciding when and what reports the marshal had to file. When some federal form relating to discrimination reached the marshal, asking him to report on "staff, broken down by age and sex," the marshal sent a note to the judge, commenting: "Age and sex ain't a real problem for us, Your Honor. It's mainly alcohol." Hodge told him to throw the form away.

Just as I had promised to get the BIA lawyers the United States attorney himself to assist their cause, I had warmed up Russell Trent pretty good for his role in moving the D.C.

trio's *pro hac vice* admission. Preparing him wasn't too hard. It was just a question of typing everything out: all capitals with double spaces so he could read it, with phonetic spelling of the big words, and salient punctuation. Russell had a way of running sentences together. As he put it so well, "When I'm reading, I'm not listening." When Russell didn't have things written out, the consequences could be dire. Bailey Sanders had noted that Russell was one of a number of lawyers "who have not mastered talking and thinking at the same time."

Getting Russell to court could be a daunting challenge. This week, official duties kept him in town—he had to receive a government check, his monthly pay. In addition, the visit of BIA officialdom from D.C. was important enough for him to make an early-morning court calendar call, so long as he did not have to do anything more substantive than move several *pro hac vice* admissions. Russell himself observed, "If there is one thing I am experienced at, it's moving the admission of the lawyers who will do the work on the case."

He later accused me of setting him up by making him argue this motion. I candidly pointed out that it was I who successfully urged against the pre-argument victory dinner he proposed for the night the BIA people arrived. My real motive in skipping this early celebration was to make sure he was available to argue his big motions. Preparing on the night before never did agree with Russell.

THE FIRST HEARING

Russell's big moment arrived. It was a Friday morning in August. We were set for a 9:30 A.M. hearing, the only civil matter on the calendar. Following this civil matter, the judge would have to pass criminal sentences on people, most of whom he knew. This did not put Judge Hodge in a happy state of mind. The Wrangell case was number one on the 9:30 call.

"*BIA versus Wrangell Point Baptists* will go over to our November Calendar," calls out Norm Filer, the clerk. Russell Trent, a little puzzled, but prepared with his boldface script, was reading forward: "*May it please the court, I have the honor to represent the United States of America and in my official capacity as United States attorney for the District of Alaska to move the admission of. . . .*"

"Russell," said the judge, "if there ain't no motion to be heard, it don't need no lawyers. Your motion just clutters the docket, and your talking lengthens the record."

"*. . . Mr. Rodgers, Mr. Straub, and Mr. Feldstein of the bars of. . . .*"

Now the judge was in a quandary. He didn't want Russell to look like an idiot in front of BIA officialdom, and he would if the judge kept interrupting him. Indeed, because Russell had earned his reputation as a defense lawyer, under stress he tended to think he was still representing defendants. Occasionally he even had to be reminded which side he was on. Russell had won a lot of cases as a defense lawyer. The Murmac Bar Association's professional assessment of that accomplishment was that jurors tended to regard having Russell Trent as your lawyer as punishment enough, therefore his clients got off.

The judge was clever at protecting Alaska lawyers' reputations. When he realized that Russell was not hearing well that day, the judge *sua sponte* (that's Latin for "all on his own") rose to the occasion on Russell's behalf: "What states did you say they were admitted in heretofore, Mr. Trent?"

"*The District of Columbia and Virginia, respectively,*"

Russell read on. Because there were one and a half secretaries working for the Department of Justice and one and a half secretaries working for the court, the judge (a believer in pretrial preparation) had obtained from the half secretary, who worked for both Russell and him, a copy of Russell's extemporaneous remarks. This enabled the judge to anticipate the questions that he could ask without throwing the U.S. attorney off the written track. Knowing Russell Trent, the judge was confident he'd stick to the script. It was a question of putting his questions at the right time.

"Mr. Rodgers is a member of the District of Columbia Bar, and Messrs. Feldstein and Straub are members of the bar of the state of Virginia. I, therefore, move their admission to the bar of the state of Alaska. Thank you, Your Honor."

"Court will be in recess while I put my thoughts in order about your motion, Mr. Trent."

"Thank you, Your Honor. I have the order prepared." Russell was starting to wing it, on his own. It was hard to guess what this portended.

"What does it say, Mr. Trent? Hand it up." Russell complied. Judge Hodge read aloud: ". . . that those lawyers are admitted to the bar of Alaska in the case of *BIA versus Wrangell Point Baptists?* Well, they are not—not yet, at least. Court is in recess for ten minutes."

"Do we have to remain, Your Honor?" Russell was already getting on to a noontime thirst and wanted to celebrate the results of his morning in court.

"Not if you and your clients don't want to. I'll just rule in accordance with the law."

"Thank you, Your Honor."

Russell was ready to leave, but lawyers Rodgers, Feldstein, and Straub were not. "What has happened, Mr. Trent?"

"The judge is going to rule," said Russell.

"Brilliant," said Feldstein. "We'll wait."

Well, wait they did. In due course, Judge Hodge reconvened, feeling pretty good about his jurisprudential instincts. "Mr. Trent, thank you for your fine presentation, and my welcome to the distinguished lawyer from the District of Columbia and to the lawyers from the state of Virginia."

"As all of you know, courts from the United States Supreme Court on up [the judge had his own priorities] are reluctant to rule on issues that aren't really before them. Now, as I understand it, what you gentlemen want is to be admitted to argue a motion that won't be heard today. Is that right, Mr. Trent?"

Russell wasn't going off any deep ends by himself with a quick yes or no to that, so he replied, "May I confer with my clients about that, Your Honor?" There was some tittering in the courtroom about this time, because it now looked as if the BIA trial lawyers were on trial. A brief conference with his "clients" was audible to all: "For Christ's sake, Trent, *yes!*" instructed Rodgers, the D.C. chief lawyer. The Judge winced at this off-the-record expletive in his courtroom, and ignored it, except to register whom it came from.

"Yes, Your Honor, if it please the court, they do."

"Well, Mr. Trent, whether or not it pleases the United States Supreme Court, I'm going to rule because you, the United States attorney for Alaska, have persuaded me to. I may be going out on a limb in ruling on a matter not really pending, in this case admitting *pro hac vice* lawyers to argue motions which won't be heard, but for the United States attorney and these lawyers coming all the way from the fine state of Virginia I'll rule, whether or not the United States Supreme Court would."

"Thank you, Your Honor."

"I rule that attorneys Feldstein and Straub of the Virginia bar are admitted *pro hac vice*. The case authorities indicate that attorneys from other states can be admitted in the federal courts of the state of Alaska, but Mr. Rodgers can't be admitted, at least at this time. The cases cited in your papers deal only with lawyers admitted in one *state* being entitled to admission in another *state*. Nothing was said about lawyers like Mr. Rodgers, from territories or whatever the District of Columbia is. We in Alaska, having been a state for only two years, remember the different kind of treatment required for a territory. The federal government had its own views in

Washington, D.C., about Alaska when it was a territory. Therefore, I can't just rush into admitting a territorial lawyer like I can a duly admitted state lawyer. Being a state is something special. I won't deny your motion for Redman today. I'll give you time for further briefing."

Rodgers was fit to be tied. As the BIA division chief, he had assembled this whole entourage, arranged the junket, and figured on a surefire win. At this point, the BIA Motion for Default Judgment had not been heard. He wasn't even sure he'd win the *pro hac vice* motion to allow him into the courthouse. On the other hand, as local legal scholars observed, he had achieved a judicial first in Alaska and maybe the whole U.S. of A. A federal judge had declined or at least deferred the admission of a federal lawyer from the federal District of Columbia in a federal court in a federal case on behalf of a federal client in a matter involving federal lands and a federal question of law. "That is," as Bailey Sanders later commented, "enough firsts to make a real reputation as a bureaucrat lawyer. No wonder Rodgers is chief of the division; he really does easy things the hard way."

The judge proceeded: "Because we'll have to give the Baptists notice of the default motion and because my own docket in Anchorage is jammed, I'm going to set this case for hearing on my Nome docket, which is quite light." The federal lawyers started to brighten at this news—maybe a quick hearing. Russell looked glum. He knew what was coming.

"However, because I'm so busy in Anchorage, I won't be able to get to Nome for some time. We'll have to set the matter for hearing in Nome the first week in January, 1962. My calendar is entirely free then." (Not his social calendar, however. Both the Judge and his wife had relatives in Nome they liked to spend Christmas with, as did his court reporter, Mable Wynot, also from Nome. A chance for all to visit their home at federal expense over the holidays was a nice present from the judge.)

"Now, Mr. Rodgers, you don't have to come to Nome if you aren't interested in being admitted to Alaska. But after

I get your supplemental brief and if I do rule for you, you'll need to be there so I can swear you in if you want to work with your associates who are now admitted to argue the default motion in Nome. Thank you for coming. Court is adjourned."

"To say that Rodgers was upset is to be ignorant of what being 'pissed off' really means" was the way Honest John Manders put it. John was known to be honest because, upon his arrival in Anchorage to practice after some contretemps with the San Francisco Bar, the sign he hung outside his office read: "John Manders, Esq. Honest Lawyer."

Three government lawyers from the nation's capital, the United States attorney from Alaska, and his staff (me) had joined forces to move for a default judgment, uncontested by the other side, who didn't even appear. Not only had we not won the motion, we couldn't even get it heard. Further than that, while all the lawyers on our side had at least found the courthouse, the court in the person of Judge Hodge hadn't found all the lawyers to be ready for Alaska federal courthouse practice.

In the local Murmac Bar's review of the day's activities, John Manders pronounced: "If this is what the Wrangell Point Baptists can do to the U.S. without lawyers and without even appearing, I think the government should start talking settlement right now."

The parting on that pleasant late-August afternoon, despite their courtroom adventures, was almost friendly. Rodgers, Straub, and Feldstein had seen a little of Anchorage. The snow was moving down the Chugach Range through green pine forests to meet the aspen trees' upward-wandering yellow farewell to summer. Cook Inlet was pristine blue. Two hundred miles in the distance the majesty of Denali—Mount McKinley, blanketed in eternal snow—could be seen. Messrs. Rodgers, Feldstein, and Straub had their appetites whetted for Alaska. They looked forward to seeing more of it on their return.

"Will we get closer to McKinley when we go to Nome?" asked Feldstein.

"Sure will," replied Russell.

"Is the scenery around Nome different?" asked Straub.

"Sure is," said Trent.

"We look forward to being back. See you in January in Nome," said Rodgers.

"Sure," said Russell Trent.

NOME

Nome in January is not a place; it is an unparalleled experience. For the three lawyers from Washington, D.C., it was another world. Rodger's naive expectation that their setting would be a happy-holiday, winter-wonderland update of the August visit had him making a lot of inquiries of Russell Trent about the trip to Nome from Anchorage. "If it is a clear day, will we be able to see McKinley?"

"Well, yes, no, and sort of" was Russell's reply. "It is clear, it is day, we will be close to McKinley, but you won't see it, because it is night all day long in January."

January day-night in western Alaska is unforgettably chilling. Nome is frozen in temperature and time. It is unnecessary to pave or to plow its streets and impossible to provide normal water or sewer service. You drive on top of the ice and snow, and beneath it the earth is iced as far as man can dig. Nome sits on the edge of the Bering strait on permafrost, with that most usual of amenities, water, having to be hauled in a heated tank truck from house to house. Conversely, sewage has to be trucked—someplace.

Life in Nome is utterly shaped by the weather. Nonetheless, it produces an ingeniously resilient populace. None of Nome's citizens are handier in managing to live in and appreciate their world than the Eskimos who made up 85 percent of Nome's year-round population.

Getting to Nome in January, 1962, was best done in the nonstop airplane owned by Arctic Airlines. It was designated the nonstop airplane because "that is God's truth," to quote Warren Cobb, the local FAA inspector. "The folks starting the airline could finance one two-engine fuselage and four engines. Airplane engines have to be inspected thoroughly every hundred hours, but the fuselage can go for ten thousand hours. To keep flying people around, they switch engines once a week, but that old fuselage goes nonstop."

For the D.C. lawyers, the trauma of leaving the bright, colored, warm interior of the Arctic Airlines plane was not merely one of psyche. They were physically afraid of Nome out of doors. The galvanized tin barn of an airport hangar-terminal loomed like some mining ghost town structure through the gray, soft white of an arctic winter day.

Snow was everywhere. The air was keen and biting from temperature and the continuous motion of omnipresent snow. Locally, there were two schools of thought about the pervasive and literal biting quality of the air. One had it that there was always snow coming down; the other, that it was frost coming up. As the marshal said, "It don't make one hell of a lot of difference which it is. It hurts like hell until you get used to it." The topic did, however, make for some good and thoughtful barroom discourse. There was a major market for that sort of intellectual exchange in Nome in the winter.

"One good thing," Russell told our assembled group, "it ain't too cold anyway, not more than fifteen below with a chill factor of minus twenty-seven. We can walk into Nome if we have to." That possibility was a real threat, for, as the marshal informed us, "People look for challenges in the humdrum of everyday life. In Nome they get plenty; just getting the car to start every day is a real challenge." So it was nip and tuck as to whether anyone from downtown Nome, about half a mile away, would be there to greet us.

The Alaska members of the entourage weren't too upset. We had the usual choice: wait or walk. Most of us had lived in Alaska for at least several winters. With some self-flattery, we considered ourselves eighty-degree people. There might even be among us a few hundred-degree folks. A minus fifteen degree walk was no big deal. By any assessment, the D.C. lawyers were at best twenty-degree people. The idea of any outside movement in the white night-gray day of Nome struck them as a numbing experience. At their request, we would wait. No one discussed their twenty-degree traits with them, but all of us recognized it as an essential measurement of human character.

The degree evaluation of newcomer Cheechakos by Alaska sourdoughs was an intellectual and real one. A "twenty-degree Cheechako" was the subject of derision that had sound basis in the reality of life in Alaska, as well as in other places where life is not temperature controlled and water doesn't come or go when you turn a handle or push a button. Getting along in the north bush country required an ability to adjust life to environment, hot or cold, clean or dirty. A hundred-degree person was a suitable companion for almost any adventure. A hundred-degree person operated at zero degrees Fahrenheit, or even minus twenty, as well as at eighty degrees above. A hundred-degree person could adjust his or her life to the world around *and function.* Conversely, the physical world dominates the twenty-degree person. Cheechakos, used to an antiseptic and air conditioned world, could operate effectively only within a temperature range of twenty degrees. For the D.C. lawyers, that range was sixty-five to eighty-five degrees Fahrenheit. In Nome in January, such a person had trouble getting out of bed. Sixty-five degrees Fahrenheit was hard to come by inside, never mind out of doors. The D.C. lawyers were twenty-degree people, and everyone knew it.

Fortunately for the D.C. lawyers, the ultimate test of their degree fortitude was obviated by the appearance of the local state trooper in his four wheeler. With a laconic "Nice day, glad to have you here," we were all bundled into the vehicle for the short trip to the North Star Hotel. Marshal Coleburn and the state police officer had worked out a mobilized co-operative sovereignty. This involved requiring the agency, state or federal, that could get its vehicles started that day to transport the other as necessary.

The North Star Hotel in Nome had a peculiar charm. Its most notable accoutrement was a life-size papier mâché cow grazing in its lobby. As with so many things and people in Nome, the cow's origins were uncertain. The tales that circulated about it, considering the space it occupied in a town where heated inside areas were always at a winter premium, made it worthwhile for advertising purposes. "It had come with a dairy farmer who could not leave all trace of his beloved Iowa behind." Or: "A 'struck-it-lucky' miner had ordered a cow for the girl of his dreams. 'Any cow, at any price,' he told a Seattle freighter captain, and he acquired a one-thousand-dollar imitation of Elsie the Borden Cow. Life working the way it does in Nome, the North Star ended up taking the cow as payment for a bar bill." At all events, money often changed hands because of ingenious wagers made with visitors about "a cow in Nome."

Room service at the North Star meant extra blankets if you were lucky. Running water came in buckets. The buckets were filled from the heated tank truck of the local water company. No pipes could be placed in the permafrost tundra. Running water was hauled in and sewage out. The utility company kept the water and sewage tanks separate, or at least rinsed them well. For those truly concerned with a healthy existence, a no-risk approach to water seemed wise. This meant bar whiskey for winter's liquid sustenance. By court call on the Monday following their arrival, Messrs. Rodgers, Straub, and Feldstein had all the North Star room service they could get and as much liquid sustenance as a twenty-degree Cheechako can handle.

The government "barrister" trio approached the heated Nome courthouse, looking forward to getting warm. This court episode couldn't involve much: Redman's *pro hac vice* admission in the federal court of Alaska, an argument, and a ruling on the government's motion to win by default because of the Wrangell Point Baptists' continued non-appearance. While Rodger's legal fate was uncertain, the default motion that brought three high-powered government lawyers from Washington, D.C., to Alaska—more precisely, to Nome, Alaska, in January, 1962—seemed a sure triumph. Two signs augured well for it: (1) the Baptists still had filed no response; (2) three government lawyers from Washington, D.C., five thousand miles away, senior lawyers, surely knew better than to risk looking foolish by losing when one local assistant United States attorney, namely *me*, could do that and be left with the choice of justifying to the Justice Department how a sure winner had een lost. It was events such as this that warmed me to the merits of bureaucratic decision-making. The Rodgers-Feldstein-Straub voyage to Nome reflected the wisdom of not letting people—government people in Washington, D.C.—vote. Without the vote they can do harm enough.

When you think of it, one federal courthouse is not all that different from the next. They can be bigger or smaller, ornate or simple, old or new. There is always a judge, a bailiff, a clerk or more, and a certain American sense of majesty about it. In fact, the Nome courthouse was 67 miles from the USSR, but not intimidated by Russia. Protected by his system, Judge Hodge made his rulings, unafraid—indeed, disdainful—of Communism or other peril. It all bespoke the inherent power of the federal judiciary. Some federal judges write great decisions, forerunners to Supreme Court wisdom. Some embark on great adventures: civil rights, integration, running school systems day in and day out. Some deal with fallen D.C.-10s, some with Agent Orange. In a wonderful combination of events, place, and time, they form our justice system. Judge Hodge in his small way, in Alaska, in Nome, in a federal courthouse, knew this.

THE NOME HEARING

"The United States of America versus the Wrangell Point Baptists," called out the marshal, acting as bailiff. Coleburn was today buckled down with his side arm, a double-ought-six pistol, should any enemy of justice appear. A double-ought-six could stop a polar bear or a grizzly. No mere man had dared to test the marshal's weapons consequences for lesser species.

"Present for the United States," said I, Russell having ceded his local-lawyer lead role, now that the script might be uncertain, "and appearing with me the United States attorney, the Honorable—"

"The what?" said Judge Hodge.

"Russell Trent," I replied.

"That's who I thought the United States attorney was," said the judge.

"—and Messrs. Feldstein and Straub from the Department of Justice also representing the government and earlier admitted by Your Honor as counsel in this case."

The courtroom was well filled. In Nome in January, a "request for a continuance, *agreed to,*" would draw a good crowd, and this case involved "a dispute, a conspiracy, and maybe the end of a religious movement."

"Crack Government Legal Team in Nome to Prevent Theft of Wrangell Point," ran the headline. "Three of the BIA's finest lawyers have followed Judge Hodge to Nome—demanding that Wrangell Point be released from domination by Christians," the story began. It continued:

> Before the judge can wrestle with the Almighty over title to land holdings, he must first address the issue of the fitness of Department of Justice attorney Rodgers to practice in Alaska courts. Judge Hodge, recognizing centuries of legal tradition, admitted two of the three government lawyers—Mr. Rodgers' underlings—to practice because they have passed state bar exams in states which recognize Alaska. Rodgers has passed no state bar exam. Judge Hodge must face the difficult problem of how to deal with what is in effect district or territorial status for lawyer Rodgers. Rodgers, a District of Columbia lawyer,

has a position akin to that of Alaska before statehood. Does a nonstate citizen have states' rights—in Alaska?

Rodgers got drunk after reading the story. This caused no upset in Nome, except that the North Star bartender said he did it on three sissy drinks, manhattans. The hapless visitor had also read:

> Once the Rodgers question is resolved, the issue of the day will be: Can the Christians living at Wrangell Point be dispossessed of their homes, church, and trap lines without a hearing in a federal court of justice? The agency in charge of protecting Native Americans and their land, the Bureau of Indian Affairs, wants to do this.

"Not an untrue word in the story," mused Judge Hodge when he read it.

The preceding quotes were all from the *Nome Nugget*. The *Nugget* had a way with local events, particularly in winter. On the basis of spectacular reporting, it regularly outsold the *National Enquirer* in Nome. This took imaginative writing and a certain flair with facts. There was not an untrue word in the *Nugget* story written on this case by Wayne Wright, the reporter locally known as "Write" Wright; but the story, factual though it was, significantly departed from reality.

Hodge did feel strongly about the BIA's ill judgment in attempting to evict the Wrangell Point Baptists. Further, he wanted the citizens of Nome to know that with the federal judiciary's backing, in appropriate causes, individual Alaskans stood as strong and tall as the government itself. Finally, the judge had a penchant for legal maneuvers that lawyers had not thought about. Taking the unanticipated legal tack made him a real judge, not just some Solomonlike dispenser of justice, offering to halve the positions of adversaries, or even ruling all the way based on the arguments of one party or the other.

With this judicial alchemist on the dais and playing to a local crowd, I was not sanguine about anything. Russell

Trent's courtroom hibernation in no way reassured me. Though Russell was no judicial scholar, he did recognize the "winter scene." A cold day in court was in store for his side, so he started hunkering down at the counsel table like a grizzly preparing for a winter slumber.

"What do you want, Lawyer Lundquist?" inquired the judge.

"May it please the court, there are two matters before you: the first, the matter of Mr. Rodgers' admission; the second, the uncontested default motion of the United States government."

"One thing at a time," replied the judge. "I have been briefed on the Rodgers admission matter, and I have studied it on my own. The government has given me a lot of precedents, but there is one great weakness in them. There is not a single Alaska decision. This will be a case of first impression here. Letting outside lawyers into Alaska courtrooms is an important matter. Further, even the precedent cases they cite are all distinguishable. Not one deals with a former territory just made a state after years of trying, recognizing right away a non-state-bar-admittee lawyer."

Rodgers was getting hot enough to thaw the adjacent Bering Sea ice cap. Feldstein and Straub dutifully looked aggrieved, although under their facial veneer they struggled between mirth and amazement at what the judge was putting their boss through.

"Because this is a judicial first for the federal district court in Alaska [since Judge Hodge was the first federal district judge in the state, he had an unrivaled record of judicial firsts there], I'll have to be careful and have a sound factual record on which to base my ruling. Bailiff, swear the witness."

"What witness, Your Honor?" I asked.

"*Your* witness, Mr. Lundquist." I was floundering but not dead in the water.

"Of course, Your Honor. Who would you like?"

"Rodgers," replied the judge.

"Oh, yes. Mr. Rodgers, please come forward and be sworn."

Rodgers, joining me in not knowing what the hell was going on, dutifully approached the bench, took the witness stand, and was sworn.

"*Your* witness, Mr. Lundquist," began Judge Hodge.

"Thank you, Your Honor, I'll proceed." I started out. Not knowing what the crafty old judge was after, but knowing him well enough to know it would make legal sense, I decided to start on firm ground.

"Your name, please, sir."

"George W. Rodgers."

"What is the W for, Mr. Rodgers?"

"Washington, George Washington Rodgers," he replied. So far, so good, I mused to myself.

"Your occupation?"

"Attorney, chief of the Legal Division, Bureau of Indian Affairs, Washington, D.C."

"How long have you held that position?"

"Two years."

"Did you go to law school?"

"Yes."

"Where?"

"Georgetown University."

"Where is that located?" interrupted Judge Hodge.

"Washington, D.C., Your Honor," replied Rodgers.

"Did you ever go to law school in a state?" asked the judge.

"No, sir."

Were we losing ground?

"Proceed, Lundquist," instructed Judge Hodge, and I proceeded, not knowing where in all of Alaska I was proceeding to.

"When did you get out of law school, Mr. Rodgers?"

"Nineteen fifty-two."

"Did you have military service?" broke in Judge Hodge.

"No," replied Rodgers. "I had an essential civilian job." No help there from good old George Washington Rodgers.

"Please tell the court, Mr. Rodgers, the history of your employment as a lawyer following your graduation from law school."

"Well, in 1952. . . ."

"Lundquist," broke in the judge, "stop this meandering. Do you think we've got all day for this? Get to the heart of the matter."

"Yes, Your Honor," I replied, not having the foggiest notion where the heart was, or for all that, what the matter was.

"May I lead the witness, Your Honor?" I inquired.

"Is he hostile?" asked the Judge.

"No, Your Honor, merely to expedite things."

"OK," said Hodge.

"Mr. Rodgers, you are here seeking *pro hac vice* admission in the case of *U.S. versus The Point Wrangell Baptists?*"

"Yes."

"On behalf of the plaintiff, United States of America, Bureau of Indian Affairs?"

"Yes."

"And do you want to be admitted to the federal district court for the District of Alaska?"

"Very much so," answered Rodgers warming to the task.

"I hope so," said the judge. "Lundquist, ask him the critical question."

"I'd like to, Your Honor, but I've misplaced it. I'd be pleased to offer Mr. Rodgers to the court for its questioning."

"Well, I dislike taking over your case, or any party's case, but I'll speed things up. Mr. Rodgers," asked the Judge, "you graduated from Law School in 1952?"

"Yes, Your Honor."

"Did you take a bar exam?"

"Yes, Your Honor."

"Did you pass it?"

"Yes, Your Honor, in the District of Columbia in 1954."

"The first time?" asked the judge. I thought of throwing in a relevancy objection, but saw it as a loser.

"No, the third," said Rodgers with some show of embarrassment at the revelation of his wanting legal scholarship, and because his earlier answer had not been 100 percent candid.

"Well," Judge Hodge said, "I'm still concerned about admitting you in Alaska, but you did finally pass one bar exam, so you are batting three-thirty-three on bar exams. My instinct about admitting foreign lawyers to practice in Alaska is to be conservative. But Mr. Rodgers, I'm going to make an exception for you." (An exception to a ruling that was to be a first!) "You're admitted—*pro hac vice*—but I hold an Alaska lawyer responsible for your conduct. I'll nominate your counsel for that—Mr. Lundquist—if he is willing. Are you willing, Lundquist?"

Between a rock and a hard place was I. "Yes, Your Honor, of course, but only if it is all right with my superior, Mr. Russell Trent."

"What do you say, Trent?" says the Judge.

"Huh?" replied Russell, now well into his hibernation.

"Can Lundquist vouch for Mr. Rodgers?" the judge persisted.

"I don't know," said Russell. "Can he?"

"He can if you'll let him," said Hodge. "Will you?"

"All right with me, Your Honor, if there is no conflict."

"Hadn't thought of that, Russell. Could be, couldn't there, if the U.S. attorney in Alaska and the BIA lawyers couldn't agree on whose justice to use?"

"Right, Your Honor, exactly what I was thinking." Russell was a courtroom survivor.

"I'm admitting him, anyway," said the judge. "I'll hold Feldstein and Straub liable if there is a problem. If there is a conflict with justice, they'll all be in contempt. Mr. Rodgers, you're under oath. Will you conduct yourself properly in our Alaska federal district court?"

"I will, Your Honor."

"You are admitted," said Hodge. "Court's in recess. We'll reconvene at 10:15."

We had a half hour to reconnoiter. There was a difference of opinion as to whether we'd won, but on balance we were persuaded by Russell's legal analysis. "Look at it this way, Mr. Rodgers, you come up here from D.C. for two motions. If this one is a win, you're batting five hundred with your folks back home, no matter what." Rodgers saw the light.

"OK, we've won this one. Now how do we handle the uncontested default?"

With the default motion filed seven or eight months ago, and the hearing on it first scheduled six months back, I was a little surprised that the BIA lawyers were going to start discussions on "how to handle it" thirty minutes before the hearing.

Russell was ready. "First, let's get a cup of coffee. We can go out to the Lazy Duck in five minutes and be back in time."

"No way," said Rodgers, although whether it was because of his respect for Nome's outdoors in January or his wanting to prepare, I had no idea.

"Larry," he said, addressing himself to Straub, "you argue the merits of the motion, and when you prevail there, I'll discuss the relief." I was surprised old Rodgers needed three tries at his bar exam. He had a sixth sense for picking, if not a sure win, at least a seemingly assured no-loss situation for himself.

"All right, Chief. Anything in particular to stress?"

"Yes, emphasize the sanctity of federal lands and the BIA's stewardship of them for the public or the Indians or whoever owns them, and don't forget, this is a default. The damned Baptists are making a fool of us and the court. They don't even come to court, and they have been living there a year rent-free."

"Yes, sir."

With that inevitable need to release nervous energy that comes up at any court-declared recess, Rodgers and Straub headed for the men's room to ease their stress. It was crowded, smoke-filled, and linguistically ababble as the predominantly Eskimo crowd assessed the situation. The entry of the D.C.

lawyers quieted things down, but not before Rodgers and Straub could overhear the *Nugget* reporter, Wayne "Write" Wright, discussing with a grizzled sourdough where the *trial* might take place.

The prospect of a real trial unsettled Rodgers and Straub considerably, and the relief obtained at the urinal was overridden by anxiety from the eavesdropping. They returned to our prep session to ask, "Trent, why are they talking about a trial?"

"Do you understand Eskimo?" asked Russell.

"No," said Rodgers.

"Then it's easy to get confused. The Eskimos might be talking about a trail."

"It was not Eskimos talking, Trent, it was the reporter and some beery old rum pot he called Frank."

"Oh, shit," said Russell. "Frank Croft must be in it." And at that moment the bailiff marshal cried, "Court's in session. *United States of America versus the Wrangell Point Baptists* for hearing."

With Trent's "Oh, shit" ringing in their ears, Rodgers and Straub, with Feldstein in tow, spread themselves out across the table in front of the judge.

"All rise, please. Court's in session, the Honorable H. Waterloo Hodge presiding." The courtroom quieted down; even the Eskimo kids stopped scampering. The big event was coming up.

I glanced at the crowd and caught the eye of Frank Croft, sitting in his duty station, the first public row, not inside the rail where members of the bar usually sat, but out in the public section. Frank was a self-styled "lawyer *of* the people"—not "against them," as he usually described attorneys for the government. Early on in Nome, Frank had used his "of the people" lawyer bit on me without malice when I had announced I was appearing on behalf of "the people" in a criminal case. "Not my people," Frank had replied; "Lundquist's against them."

Following that trial, Frank had explained at length to me that his "lawyer of the people" role was one of the major reasons he had established himself as the premier lawyer of the Nome-Kotzebue bar. He knew all the citizens there and was inevitably representing one of the people. He was also the only lawyer resident in that area. As the sole lawyer in Nome, he almost got himself a Martindale Hubbell *av* rank. Every lawyer in Alaska reporting on him said, "Frank Croft is the best lawyer in Nome and Kotzebue." Martindale got hung up when it came to establishing Frank's credit rating. John Manders had reported, "Good at the North Star bar, not so good elsewhere." Bailey Sanders had replied, "So far as I can determine, Mr. Croft has always been able to get credit," but that didn't quite do it for Messrs. Martindale and Hubbell. Frank got only a *bv* rating.

Whatever his rating elsewhere, in Nome—where he was "of the people" because that's where he kept up on current law and current events—he was "the best." Indeed, Frank knew from his discussions with the local Nome TV critics— that group constituting everyone who didn't spend 80 percent of the time in a bar—which stateside television legal defenses were in vogue for potential juries and what they expected for a win in court. Indeed, John Manders said he preferred Frank Croft's in-court reruns of Perry Mason's defenses to the acted-out television make-believe stuff. Frank wasn't always able to get a confession from someone in the back row of the courtroom, but he often came close. However you considered it, Frank Croft in a Nome courtroom was powerful medicine.

Straub and Rodgers had no inkling of this. They didn't even know the Wrangell Christian Baptists had a lawyer. Judge Hodge did, because he saw Frank in his duty spot, drowsing a little after a couple of midmorning beers but ready for action.

"The hearing on the government's motion for a default judgment and an order of eviction for the Wrangell Point Baptists is now before me. Who is handling it for the government?"

"We are," said Rodgers. "Mr. Straub will explain why a default judgment must be ordered in this case, and I—"

"Did you say *must*, Mr. Rodgers?"

"Yes, Your Honor."

"I thought so," said the judge. "Proceed."

"—and I, Your Honor, will explain the nature of the eviction remedy the default entitles us to."

"Wait a minute, Mr. Rodgers. Before we get to remedies, we have to deal with rights of the people and *responsibilities* on the government's part."

"Yes," said Rodgers nervously. "Perhaps I should sit down and let Mr. Straub argue the default."

"Well, anyway, it would be good if you sat down," said the judge, "and by the way, where is the place for the defendants' lawyer? You three have taken over the entire counsel table."

"We thought, Your Honor, that we could use it all to spread out, for the Wrangell Point Baptists don't have a lawyer."

"If I might start on the default argument," began lawyer Straub.

"I don't know," said Hodge.

Then Frank's voice sang out from his seat just beyond the courtroom rail: "*Not guilty,* Your Honor, is the plea the Baptists enter. Not guilty to all fifty-seven counts, and affirmatively we plead the First Amendment and counterclaim for damages, both special and general, real and personal."

"I'm Frank Croft, Your Honor, duly admitted, *the first time I tried,* to this Alaska court. I'm appearing for all the Wrangell Point Baptists, and also *in rem* for their land and all God's creatures on it."

"Would you like to have a seat at the defense table, Mr. Croft?"

"Not if it would in any way crowd out the government lawyers, and their need for space, Your Honor. I can do fine from here."

"Your appearance is noted and the plea entered, Mr. Croft. Go on, Mr. Straub."

Straub was dead in the water, and the lake was frozen over. He didn't know what hit him or where he was shot, but he did sense it was mortal insofar as any default judgment was concerned.

Fatally wounded, but game, he went on.

"Your Honor, for over one year the Wrangell Baptists have invaded government land, shot its game, taken its fish—"

"Your Honor," said Frank, "if it's illegal hunting, why, I add to our affirmative pleas that my clients are duly licensed and have permits and shoot only in season except for allowable sustenance shooting, all of which this court is very familiar with."

"It's not a matter of illegal hunting, Your Honor, it's—"

"Then why bring such things up, Mr. Straub, in a default hearing?" said the judge.

"Yes, Your Honor, it's a default, and for seven months the government and the court have been defied. We know the Baptists have been served. This court's processes have been violated; there has not been so much as a pleading filed. The government is being flouted."

"Well," said Hodge, "you ought to be real pleased that you're not being flouted today, that they have acceded to what the government wants and come to court. Aren't you pleased you've won so far, Mrs. Straub? Aren't you Mr. Rodgers?"

Their respective silences were apoplectic.

"What should we do now?" said Hodge.

Straub, still fighting: "Your Honor, there is no paper on file, nothing."

"They plead not guilty, Mr. Straub, and if that oral response is good enough to tell the government what is going on in a criminal case, it sure should be good enough for a civil case."

"But there are affirmative pleadings we'll file, Your Honor," said Frank.

"Write" Wright, in reporting on it later, wrote:

With that response the momentum of the legal game shifted. The puck had been passed down the ice to Frank Croft—and he was some stick handler. He was ready to make his moves, and quick, and proceeded to do so, saying, 'Your Honor, I apologize. I just got the case last night when Mrs. Inizua of Wrangell Point flew in with a $25 retainer. I couldn't get no affirmative pleading done, but I'll have it tomorrow so you can start the trial today. I don't think it's more than a one-dayer for the government, and by tomorrow my pleading and my witnesses will be here. . . .'

It was indeed Frank's move.

"Trial?" said Rodgers. "Trial?" said Straub. "Trial?" said Feldstein.

"Trial. Why not?" said Judge Hodge. "We didn't set the Nome session for seven days without expecting we might have to do business, and your trial is our only business."

"Ready for the defense," said the ever-helpful Frank Croft.

Rodgers: "We're not ready, Your Honor. Trial . . . trial now . . . impossible."

"Not ready?" said Judge Hodge. "You filed in June, last year. You've investigated, you got fifty-seven pages of complaints not even counting motions, you got three BIA lawyers and the whole United States attorney's office for all Alaska. You come five thousand miles to Nome and you are not ready! I should enter a nonsuit against the plaintiffs and get this long-pending case off my calendar—both calendars: It's pending in Anchorage and Nome. Both my rules and the Federal District Rules call for the prompt and efficient resolution of disputes. If the government of the U.S.A. and the Bureau of Indian Affairs won't do that, how can we expect individual citizens to respect our laws?"

Trent and I, sitting in the lawyers' row near the rail, whispered to Frank: "Come on, Frank, go easy. Maybe we can work it out. And besides, you don't want to win too quick."

Whether it was his judgment that the time wasn't right or the punishment not yet sufficient for the crime, legal courtesy, or the influence of a recession in Frank's legal economic marketplace, Frank turned into sweet reason.

"Your Honor, if you are willing, we won't push for trial. We'll let the government have more time to try to come up with something. I won't fight a continuance, but my clients should not have to pay needless money so the government can get its day in court. If we get expenses for Mrs. Inizua's travel here, my fees and expenses, money for me to come to the next trial, we'll let it continue."

"Well," began Judge Hodge.

"Your Honor, that is an outrage," said Rodgers. (Trent, quietly to me: "Shit.")

"You mean you are outraged Frank doesn't want you nonsuited?"

"No, the continuance, the costs and fees."

"Mr. Rodgers, I don't understand you. You are an uncharitable man. Too bad you never practiced in any state court. It might have taught you courtesy. You wanted to be admitted in Alaska, and I admitted you."

"Yes, Your Honor."

"You wanted the Wrangell people to appear in the case."

"Yes, Your Honor."

"And they appeared. You knew the U.S. of A. is not entitled to relief without proving its case."

"Yes, Your Honor."

"And now you don't want a trial with five U.S. lawyers here and the Wrangell Christians ready to go."

"We don't want trial now, Your Honor."

"You have spent a lot of government money in this case, Mr. Rodgers, a lot."

"Yes, Your Honor."

"And you are still not ready to try it *now*. Mr. Croft says, OK, continue it for the U.S. of A., but not at the expense of his Christian clients."

"Yes, Your Honor."

"Don't you think it would be reasonable, therefore, for the government to pay the small cost of one lawyer fee and a few witnesses for local travel and expense, when defendants will agree to continue the case at your request?"

"Yes, Your Honor."

"So stipulated," said the judge, knowing he had eliminated that appeal point, "but, Frank, keep your costs in line, I'll be watching."

"Certainly, Your Honor, we won't outspend the Government. I always stay at the Arctic Inn, four to a room and—"

"Never mind, Frank. When can we try the case? Mr. Filer, how's next June in Anchorage?"

"Fine, Your Honor."

"June 12 it is," said the judge. "See you there. Court's adjourned."

As the crowd flowed out, Frank came over to be introduced to the government team and to congratulate the government lawyers on all the winning points the judge gave them.

Rodgers, Straub, and Feldstein were terse. Frank asked, "Can I have a few weeks to file my counterclaim, Russell?" We agreed. No one was going to Hodge on that one.

"I look forward to seeing you in Anchorage in June, then," said Frank, "but just to show I'm no poor loser here in my hometown, I'll buy a drink to celebrate your continuance victory."

The D.C. lawyers looked as if they'd rather die first, or at least drink Nome recycled water. Old Russell Trent had the answer. "Sure, we will, and there is no conflict in the defense lawyer buying for the Justice lawyers. The judge has ordered that we pay your expenses, so the U.S. of A. is going to pay the whole damn bill. I'll drink to that." We all did.

ABOUT THE TRIAL

Rare is the community that doesn't respond to a major trial. People are interested; there is controversy, someone wins, someone loses; fortunes, homes, and freedom can be involved. *BIA v. The Wrangell Point Christian Baptists* involved all of these. In addition, Anchorage lacked for major events. It is a city, Alaska's major city, but until recent revisions it sat as many as five time zones away from points in the Lower

Forty-Eight, and indeed two time zones away from Alaska's capital city, Juneau. People in Anchorage felt a sense of frustration in wanting to be city dwellers in the state's only metropolis, while at the same time being embarrassed about that feeling because they also want to feel they live at the frontier's edge. So, big doings were sought after and, if need be, created. Any event that would confront frontier values, Christianity, and bureaucrats didn't need any "making up." This trial had all the trappings of a good fight.

Further, as Joe Slade, the Murmac bartender, observed, nothing had happened in Anchorage since the February Fur Rendezvous with its World Dogsled Championships. There are only so many ways to discuss the thrills of a forty-six mile dog race. Throughout the spring they had all been covered, reviewed, and re-reviewed. Joe put it well: "The town is ready for action."

By this time, the Washington lawyer trio of Rodgers, Feldstein, and Straub had been fondly labeled: Lawyers Reel, Fall, and Stumble. It was widely conceded that through effort, paperwork, and government training they had taken a medium good government lawsuit and turned it into a disaster. To pull the case their way, to make it a winner, required an absolute lead-pipe cinch legal theory that Judge Hodge could not get around, even if he so desired. The general feeling was that the judge had such a desire. The Murmac bar view was that, unfortunately for the Wrangell Point folks, the BIA had a case that was legally solid even beyond judicial emotion.

The government did own the land. Settling or even squatting on it was against the law. There could not be adverse possession against the government. There was some thought that maybe the government had title problems, but Fiddle at the local BIA office had proudly determined that the Statehood Act in literal terms had granted the United States express title to *this* land.

The Murmac Bar Association put a lot of thought into what defense old Frank Croft might come up with. Bailey Sanders, who had had the best of the earlier theoretical Nome defense strategies, was pushing for a *ferae naturae* trappers'-right approach. As he described it, "If the law says you can't own wild animals, then the land on which they reside can't be owned. So long as the Baptists keep fishing and trapping, it is within the *res gestae* of the *ferae naturae* rights that they can stay there." While there was respect for this argument's ingenuity and its employment of Latin terms, no one thought it a winner. Bailey's legal support for it came in a Kansas case that was a "matched bay mare" to this situation. Unfortunately, as often happened with Bailey's authorities, he could not find the citation.

Honest John Manders, the only other devoted legal scholar, opted for a First Amendment freedom-of-religion defense. "God put them there, and you can't interfere with God," advised John.

There was genuine respect for the fact that Frank Croft would come in well prepared with theories of his own. The Nome law library was old and had few books. Frank was well acquainted with all of them. This ability to have hands-on contact with all the law in town had often given Frank the advantage over lawyers visiting Nome, as had his disposition to possess on loan all the law books that contained his authorities, making it difficult for opponents to distinguish the "authoritative" cases he used to support his legal positions. In addition, Frank had reviewed his courtroom performances time and again with every juror who had ever sat in a trial in Nome. He knew the thinking of bush people and what appealed. This bush knowledge was, however, thought to be a mixed blessing in Anchorage, with its cosmopolitan affectations.

The D.C. lawyers still felt they were being rushed to trial. Fifty-seven-page complaints were easy to write, as were uncontested motions. Actually trying a case was a once-or-twice-a-career experience for them. Collectively, the trial experience for this team added up to a cipher. Ironically, we members of the local U.S. of A. team had tried so many cases that they blurred in recall. We thought of cases not so much in terms of individual trials but rather as categories. Crimes of violence: "A-and-B's" (simple assault and battery), "murders 1, 2, or 3" (i.e., premeditated, manslaughter, or involuntary homicide). Or complex crimes like tax evasion: for example, "didn't-files," "hidden-income," "two-books," "net-worth," and so on. Likewise, the defenses were categorized as "didn't-do-its," "didn't-mean-to-do-its," or "If-I-did-it-it-didn't-hurt-nobody." And, of course, in the Alaska terminal-divorce cases, always a woman shooting a man, the "he-was-mean-to-me" defense had been a consistent winner. There were simply too few women for courts to put one out of circulation, just for shooting a husband. On the other hand, there were more than enough husbands to go around. It also made the property settlements (which the judges disliked fussing with) very simple—survivor takes all.

That June, Anchorage was at its best. Everything was green, and the sun was working on chlorophyll production almost around the clock. People had slept enough in the winter to stay active twenty hours a day. Spring in the far north, with the sun always there, always close to the horizon, almost touchable, instills excitement. A spirit of rebirth is at hand. The cold ground of a month past is now resplendent with big flowers, doing their damnedest to outbloom each other twenty-four hours a day. The surging wilderness affects and infects the human condition. The frontier and the old dreams are bright again. The winter heart skips a beat into the pace of the arctic spring-summer madness.

The Point Wrangell Baptists came to town blooming with a renewed sense of their religion. God had brought them to Point Wrangell. As sure as God knew what he was doing, justice would prevail.

On the first day in court, Frank Croft entered the fray assuming it would be a jury trial. As he put it: "It's a crime to take a person's land away, or if it ain't, it should be. Since the government wants to take my client's land, we have a right to a jury trial, guaranteed by the Constitution in all criminal-type cases." Hodge thought this persuasive; Reel, Fall, and Stumble thought it a nightmare. It was one thing to have a trial in the first fifteen or twenty years of their government law practice, but for that to be a jury trial would give them collectively more experience than the entire BIA legal department had experienced in the last decade. The whole idea was too heady for their lawyer's souls. Besides, they were suing under statutes that had always involved cases tried before a judge.

"Write" Wright, who had wangled an expense paid trip from the *Nome Nugget* to cover the trial, wrote the *Nugget* headline. It also made the national news, for "Write" had Associated Press stringer status to report Alaska legal matters. "Bureau of Indian Affairs Does Not Care What People Think," led his story of the government attack on use of a jury. In fact, old Frank had made much of that point in court when he asked Rodgers point-blank, "If the taxpayers are paying your government salary, why don't you want any of our citizens in the jury box to see the kind of work you do?"

Meanwhile, Hodge had taken his own fancy to the jury approach for this case. It would mean he might personally avoid the hard decisions. He kept his own pressure on the BIA by calling a jury venire in for impaneling on the second day of trial. Rodgers, in a last effort to head this off, started rhapsodizing about how complex the case was. As we could have told him, if he had asked, this was entirely the wrong approach with Judge Hodge, for if the case were complex, he would surely favor letting the jury wrestle with the facts so he could keep his head clear for simple law matters.

"You brought an eviction action, didn't you, Mr. Rodgers?" asked the judge. "To throw the defendants off their land?"

"Well, yes," conceded Rodgers, "but there are many other points in our case."

"Fifty-seven pages' worth," the judge muttered. "Are you out to make it complicated?"

"No, Your Honor."

"Well, then, why can't people understand it? Your defense looks like lawyer trickery to me. My disposition is to start with a jury tomorrow."

Absolute BIA panic prevailed. "What do we do, Trent?" they gasped.

"Try the case," Russell offered.

This news totally shook them out of their native habitat of government manuals, regulations, and etceteras. Rodgers resorted to the only thing he could think of and wired Washington for advice. The reply was quick and merciful, although soon known to all, for it came telexed, and the marshal makes public records public. "Read the statute," said the telex, "para sub(b) part 26, 'there is no right of jury trial in cases in which the government asks to protect its rights to government property.'"

The next day didn't start too well. The jury panel was there, and Rodgers wanted an in-chambers conference with Judge Hodge. The judge would have none of that and said, "It is all to be on the record, Mr. Rodgers."

Rodgers fed the judge the statute, real slow, trying to suppress a smile. Hodge was apoplectic. "Why didn't you tell me that yesterday?" he sputtered. "We spent a whole day arguing the matter, and you either didn't know the law or if you did, you didn't tell me the law. This isn't even some state court law, which I know you have an excuse for not knowing. I should hold you in contempt for something. Look at all the citizens kept from their work because of you. They're brought in for a government jury trial, and now you tell me the government's law is against that!"

In fact, that jury hadn't worked in a long, long time, from the looks of it. Its members were relishing inside work and the daily fee for beer money. "Because of your holding back the law, Mr. Rodgers, I'm awarding a week of jury fees to each juror, because they came here for the Wrangell Point people. Don't you think that's fair?"

"Yes," said chief counsel Rodgers, sheepishly.

The jurors were overjoyed and much indebted to the Wrangell people for the government's munificence. One of them observed, as quoted in "Write's" column, "It is only a little civic action, such as the work of the Wrangell Christians, that can get the gd U.S. government to do any funding of Alaskans."

As the snow flower pushes up amid the last white drifts of winter to take its first proud look for the life that will soon come brightly forth around it, so did the Wrangell Christians' trial bring the new life of spring to Anchorage. While all the roads in Anchorage did not lead to the courthouse, the three paved ones did. First Street, on which the courthouse sat, and the two streets east and west were the only paved bridges across the muddy trails that otherwise served as roads.

Down one of these paths from Point Wrangell and Lake Louise came the Baptists. Their trail, the Glenn Highway, constituted a tributary of the Alcan Highway. When the Baptists left Lake Louise, 150 miles northeast of Anchorage, winter was still with them. The road was gelid. But by the time they reached the Matanuska Valley, winter was in retreat.

The farms of Matanuska are framed against the vertically steep jagged mountains. The valley begins its yearly rebirth with the labor pains of springtime farming in Alaska. For some of the Baptists, the old Polish ones, this valley had been home for many years. They looked for open latch strings for friends to meet with. They found them.

The Reverend himself lacked friends in both Matanuska and Anchorage. Manders speculated that the Reverend was "skittish" about publicity. His California notoriety as a "God-blessed" real estate salesman wasn't going to be much help with Judge Hodge.

The Reverend's "pack" was another matter. Skittish they might also be, but it was the skittishness of a he-cub spoiling for a rough time on his first outing from the winter den. Like young bears they emerged from the confines of hibernation at Lake Louise; mother's-milk-fattened and ready for life.

The Wrangell folks had a clumsy attractiveness. Dull clothes, but bright faces. Lively, spirited, good-feeling people, ready to work hard for their livelihood and to share the fruits of their labor with others. They would be tough to convince that God was wrong in his dealings with them and that the U.S. government was right, so they'd have to lose their homes to the BIA. The Murmac Bar Association knew Hodge would have trouble with that concept, too. One way or another, his judging work in Alaska would be marked by this precedent.

Thumper Johnson, the instigator of the whole Point Wrangell legal hassle, came to town reluctantly under government subpoena. While he wanted the Wrangellers out of his homeland, to testify for the BIA was "trading with the enemy." Thumper Johnson, too, would be remembered for his part in this trial. In the bush it is best to be remembered as a friend.

Helpfully for Thumper's morale, his own informant network (in the person of Tom Square of the Alaska Railroad, who had a lot of freight contact with the Baptists) disclosed to him that the Wrangellers weren't mad at Thumper. They could understand mortal differences, envy, and even men's squabbles over land. The Reverend had indeed made his California poke by playing to just such human values. But for the government, which could put "In God We Trust" on its nickels, to set up a whole BIA agency to work against that "trust" really made it an agent of the Devil.

Right out front as the Devil's agents were Rodgers, Feldstein, and Straub, paraded around town by the ubiquitous Fiddle. They had made the mistake *"again,"* as John Manders noted, of "being persuaded by their own briefs." There was no jury to contend with, just law. Manders commented, "God knows they have enough law for three cases. The entire Department of Justice must have spent all winter working on this one case. If they lose, the BIA can go out of business in Alaska."

Not content with its own legal brainwashing, the Reel, Fall, and Stumble firm was being pushed by Fiddle into seeking to brainwash the local populace with the soundness of the government's cause. Fiddle became their PR flack. Increasingly, they spent time on radio interviews and with newspaper reporters at the expense of last minute trial preparation. Frank Croft himself often directed reporters to them as "the people with the real news in this case."

The BIA trio must have assumed that Judge Hodge personally followed his jury instruction about "not reading newspapers or talking with others about the case when you're out of the courtroom." This was an instruction old Hodge gave juries only when pressed, for he knew it was the one certain way to provoke the jurors to read out of court accounts of a case.

"Write" Wright had a field day. The AP wire service, the *Nome Nugget*, and even the *Anchorage Times* were using his special interviews. "Mr. Rodgers, 'a senior solicitor' with the all-powerful Bureau of Indian Affairs, disclosed to this reporter that all the law and all prior courts have held for his agency in matters like this. 'The land is ours,' Rodgers said, 'to manage as our agency decides. The statehood sovereignty of Alaska has nothing to do with it.' " Hodge sure smarted over that one.

When asked about the Lord's direction to the Baptists, Feldstein had said, "Christian Gods have nothing to do with this case. The law is for the government."

Fiddle, trying to hold up his own end of the local public relations effort, said he had spent "eighteen months researching the title to the land and it belongs to the U.S. of A., *fee simple*." This, as explained by Wright, based on his interview with Fiddle meant that "the government simply didn't have to pay any fee, but could simply take land, pay no taxes, and in fact tax others to pay the salaries of the government agents who run the land, as they saw fit."

Marshal Coleburn said the conduct of the D.C. trio-plus-one reminded him of a long-past criminal trial in Nome involving a claim jumper. The defense lawyer, some fancy San Francisco dude, got the town so riled up by his defense of claim jumping that when the hue and cry went up in Nome to get the guilty, and the lynch mob started out with its rope in search of quick justice, the mob chased the lawyer, not the client. "Generally speaking," said Coleburn, "that sort of lawyer conduct makes for a tough day in court."

As far as the court was concerned, I knew Judge Hodge was troubled about this case and was playing it close to his robe. My office was effectively Hodge's convenience store, so I saw a lot of him. He was usually talking to himself about cases, thereby giving me hints about his judicial process. On this case, he had turned inward and was apparently bothered. His secretary, Thelma Square (Tom's wife), said the old man must be thinking of the fall hunt. He was map-happy, looking for the best hunting and fishing land in the state.

The government strategy was simple enough: just prove it owned the land. Then the law was all on its side when it came to the question of control. People can't live on government land. People can't squat on it. People can't adversely possess it. People can go on it only with a government permit when the government says so.

Frank Croft knew the government had a strong case. To get the Point Wrangell case going, Frank needed good live testimony. While he had a church full of Baptists to get things steamed up, he really needed some help from government witnesses under cross-examination.

The Murmac Bar reviewers thought the government had a "lay down" case: just introduce the title to the land, one certified copy of the pertinent map dealing with Alaskan statehood, then relax. But they were equally confident that

Reel, Stumble, and Fall were too city-smart to do that. In fact, "Write" Wright had had a little liquid coaching from Frank (Frank had long believed in spending defense monies on reporters, but only to make certain they reported fair). There was nothing wrong with accepting drinks, in "Write" Wrights's view: "After all, we are a free press." At all events, in his interviews with the government's middle-aged neophyte trial team, Wright had inquired a good bit about demonstrative evidence, live witnesses, and trial strategy. Its lawyers had been expansive in telling what the government's case would be. As a consequence, the BIA solicitors were publicly committed in Wright's articles to calling Thumper, "who had been a witness to the crime of Christians living and working peacefully together." Fiddle, who had researched the title, and old Doc Pierce, who had flown some aerial map pictures, were also witness candidates, and maybe even one or two Christian Baptist defendants would be called as hostile witnesses to prove they were there.

With Wright's pre-trial free-press discovery on behalf of the Wrangell Christians, Frank was assured of some targets to shoot at, even if he didn't know yet what game he was out to bag. As an experienced criminal defense lawyer, Frank was content to develop his case as the government's went along.

THE TRIAL

The Anchorage federal courtroom steamed as a human caldron. In front of the court rail, the Anchorage bar—John Manders, Bailey Sanders, Wendell Kay, and other senior members—held good seats. There was a tacit "court holiday" everywhere in town, except in Hodge's courtroom.

The local press, knowing well the strength of its freedom and the primacy of its constitutional rights, had worked out arrangements to take over the jury box for itself, now that the judge was deciding the case. "After all, " as Stella Reeves of the *Anchorage News* explained to Marshal Coleburn, who controlled the seating arrangements, "the First Amendment does come *first*." The marshal knew exactly what she meant.

The courtroom spectators were as variegated as Alaska itself. Seven or eight Eskimo patients from the Native Hospital, still winter parkaed, sat quiet, virtually immobile, used as they were to the white man's blessings—in their case, tuberculosis. There were bushmen, in from gold claims and trap lines; bush farmers, who loved the land they daily fought against; the loners, almost hermits, renegades from society who were reluctant to visit cities, fearing what whiskey and women and other men of strong disposition did to them or caused them to do. Marshal Coleburn and the local police chief granted an informal amnesty to the bushmen who made the trip to check out this trial. The courtesy was similar to the one practiced when a witness came to town to testify in one case even while wanted in another. Such witnesses were allowed to come in and cooperate with the system while in town, then were given one day's head start on their way back to the bush.

Bush telegraph, word of mouth and countless ham radio operators had the news out: The BIA was out to oust the Baptists. The government said the wild Point Wrangell land was theirs—a position hardly in favor with those who believed wilderness could not be owned. The bush practice was to use land, carefully not fouling the nest, then to move on. Bush folks treated the tender earth of the north with respect. For some, the Point Wrangell folks might ordinarily be considered intruders and not favored. However, with the BIA against them, all sentiment went their way.

Thumper Johnson was considerably nervous about the bushmen. They wouldn't know that the Wrangell folks had granted him a Christian Forgiveness. The bush response to his testimony could have an impact on his shipping business at the minimum. At the maximum, like Thumper's wife, "He could get lost on the way to his dentist," according to Tom Square.

Each of the bushmen looked big. Whatever their physical size, life in the bush in and of itself requires stature. Needless to say, they were all hundred-degree people. Used to weather and hunger, inured to pain, a broken leg, an ax cut, toothaches, illness, they knew these were matters to deal with *alone*. In the main, they lived too far apart to develop friendships, though they knew of one another. A few other trappers, a general-delivery address at Talkeetna or Willow, and Doc Pierce's occasional fly-in were enough links to civilization for them. They learned from Doc Pierce where each ranged, and they respected one another's territorial imperatives. With spring breakup and the special issue of this trial—the BIA against their land—they were drawn to the Anchorage federal courthouse.

Then there was the Wrangell crowd, the thirty-six who could come and be seated in the first six rows nearest the jury box: Polish immigrants, California real estate hucksters, farmers, with strong wilderness wives. These women delivered children, food, nursing, and hard work. Their profession was turning cabins into homes and children into citizens. With them were bright-faced children, so perfect in looks and deportment that they could have stepped from a Norman Rockwell painting. The Murmac barristers admired Frank Croft's choice of clients. "Leave it to old Frank, he's got a cast of clients ready for a Broadway run. When he's through, there won't be a dry eye in the house unless Frank wants one." Even the Reverend Doheney was as close to just right as a used car salesman turned land robber turned minister could be.

"Call the case Marshal," said Judge Hodge. Coleburn himself had become bailiff for this trial.

"The Bureau of Indian Affairs a/k/a BIA" (Coleburn couldn't resist showing a little criminal law expertise) *"of the United States of America"* (this subtly communicated reproach produced a whispering shift of postures in the Courthouse audience indicating distaste that the U.S. of A. and the BIA Agency were aligned) *"versus the Point Wrangell Baptists and the One Hundred Doe Defendants,* in an action of ejectment."

"Ready, Your Honor for the Plaintiff United States of America," intoned Rodgers.

"Ready for the Baptists," retorted Frank.

"Mr. Rodgers," said the judge, "who are the Does?"

"The Does, Your Honor, why I don't know. That's why we named Does."

"You want them evicted?" asked the judge.

"Yes, Your Honor, we'll prove—"

"Wait a minute, Mr. Rodgers. How can I even theoretically evict unknown people?"

"Well, Your Honor—"

"Do you know where you want them evicted from?"

"Yes, Your Honor, we'll prove—"

"You know the place where you want to evict unknown people from, but you don't know the people?"

"Yes, but—"

"Coleburn . . . Marshal Coleburn," inquired Hodge, "have you ever evicted unknown people?"

"It ain't in the Marshals' Manual, Your Honor, and if it ain't there, I ain't done it. The Department of Justice publishes the manual."

"The same Department that Rodgers works for, Marshal?"

"I believe so, Your Honor."

"I'll be damned," said the judge, although of course Mable Wynot, the court reporter, didn't hear that.

"Are the unknown Does Baptists, Mr. Rodgers?"

"Yes, Your Honor, it is just that—"

"Marshal, does the manual deal with evicting unnamed Baptists?"

"No, Your Honor."

"Well, this is sure a hell of a problem."

"Mable Wynot got that "hell" down as "heck.""

"Proceed, Mr. Rodgers," said the judge, "but bear in mind you have a very substantial problem on which I'll want briefing—short briefs, Rodgers—if you couldn't know the defendants names, in fifty-seven pages of writing a complaint. Maybe a short brief will do it."

"May I proceed with my opening?"

"Opening? Opening?! A fifty-seven page complaint. No jury, hundreds of pages of law, Doe defendants you don't know, and you want to open too. How long?"

"Half a day perhaps, a little more" said Rodgers.

"Half a day," said the judge. "Frank, will you open, too?"

"We already pled not guilty, Your Honor. That's it for us!" Frank had no interest in an opening statement. He had no idea of what the defense was until the plaintiff's case revealed its own weaknesses and strengths.

"Mr. Rodgers, has the government set forth what your case is about in your pleadings?"

"I hope so, Your Honor."

"You do expect I read the pleadings?" For the judge, that was a no-lose question.

"Yes, sir."

"Don't 'Sir' me Mr. Rodgers. This is not the army. Just plain 'Your Honor' is fine."

"Yes, Your Honor."

"No openings," said the judge. "I don't care how careless the government is with our money. I won't let them spend it recklessly in my court. I'll save them lawyers' time despite themselves. I don't need to hear and read the same thing. Call your first witness, Rodgers."

In the barristers' row there was a quiet whisper to the effect that "old Frank Croft's starting out to try one helluva case," as Rodgers squeaked out, "My—our first witness is Mr. Fiddle, Your Honor."

Horace Fiddle, Esq., BIA lawyer for years, mired for a lifetime in the drab service of government work, faced his first chance at glory. He had started with the government after graduating from night law school in the late 1930s, then passed wartime service years as a government lawyer moving Japanese Americans around the United States. He was too valuable for regular military service because he did the legal work involved in confiscating the land of California's Japanese farmers, World War II's "Yellow Peril," and relocating them. For Horace, that work was as close to peril as the world war had ever brought him. Then it was back to D.C. to apply his legal skills, developed in taking property and interning Japanese Americans, to BIA purposes in managing Indians and their land. Then, as a last wild fling, after twenty-seven years of government laboring, he was promoted or exiled (depending on one's point of view) to Alaska to run the BIA's legal shop in Anchorage. In over thirty years of government service (which involved cumulatively between two and four years of normal human productive work), this was his first headliner court experience. As Fiddle told his wife and others, this time he would participate as a lawyer, as a witness, and in a "sure-win case."

Incredibly to the members of the assembled Anchorage trial bar, Rodgers took an inordinate time to draw Fiddle out on his qualifications, especially the wartime service part: "Locking up the Japanese and taking their land." (Feldstein had briefed Rodgers on bringing out the wartime experience of experts. But Feldstein's research hadn't indicated that you developed your witnesses' wartime experience *only if it were favorable*.)

Judge Hodge still limped from German shrapnel acquired in France during World War I. He had grown up with Native American Eskimos in Nome and knew of their foreign treatment by the U.S. government. Rodgers' questioning of Fiddle evoked from that fair jurist an antipathy toward Fiddle that far exceeded Hodge's normal dislike of BIA employees.

After about a one-hour development by Rodgers of Horace Fiddle's tainted war record, Baily Sanders felt that Rodgers was deliberately taking away much of Croft's cross-exam. If he was, Rodgers' antics at the recesses didn't indicate he knew it. "Going in great, isn't it, Trent?" he asked the United States attorney. "Not even an objection from Croft."

Russell muttered, "Maybe he don't need to."

Rodgers was so flushed with being at courtroom center stage that he was as oblivious to the effect of Fiddle's testimony as was Fiddle himself. John Manders observed, "A mediocre law-

yer or expert witness is one who thinks the judge is listening to
every word when he isn't, but it's the really lousy lawyer who
doesn't realize the judge *is* listening to every word and getting
madder by the syllable." Hodge was.

The merits part of Fiddle's testimony dealt with title to the
Point Wrangell land, proving that the government owned it.
Rodgers had three choices. He could ask the judge to look
at the law, the act that created the state of Alaska and mapped
out what land the U.S. of A. owned. This would end the
case on a legal ruling. Or, he could introduce a certified copy
of the actual land transfer deed, which Fiddle had with him
on the stand. The final choice would be to have Fiddle testify
about the land title as a land expert. One and two were
simple, so Rodgers opted for using Fiddle as an expert.

"Live testimony is best," Feldstein advised him from something he had read.

"They are trying this case using the chapter headings in
a course book for trial lawyers," Trent told me. Where he
had ever seen such a book was a mystery. I believed Russell, though, because I knew he could read the large print
chapter headings. That was the one part of legal books he
did look at. Further, the United States attorney had learned
that it was hard to present too simple a case. Ignoring that
wisdom, Rodgers began the government's important testimony.

"Mr. Fiddle," inquired Rodgers, "what have you been asked
to prepare yourself for as an expert in this case?"

"Objection," said Croft.

"Sustained," said the judge.

"Why?" asked Rodgers.

"What is the basis of your objection, Frank?" asked the
judge.

Frank, who wasn't used to dealing with lawyer interro-
gation or offering legal reasons for his objections, paused for
a moment, then asked: "Can I have the question read back,
Your Honor?"

"Of course."

After the reading: "Objection, Your Honor," said Frank.

"But Your Honor, he is surely qualified as his testimony has established," said Rodgers, "he is an experienced government lawyer, knowledgeable about land titles, and has testified he has researched this title. He is qualified."

"What do you say to that, Frank?"

"It ain't qualifications, Your Honor. Anyone who has taken land from Japanese Americans and put them in concentration camps is surely a U.S. government expert on land title. It's relevance.

"If Mr. Fiddle can give his views on that, so can the Reverend and his pack, probably Thumper Johnson, old Skookum Jim, who is here and who has prospected around Wrangell for thirteen years, Doc Pierce, who flies over it, Deputy Larson, who finally found it, and on and on. The people named have at least been on the land, and Fiddle ain't." (Frank had done some informal discovery in the BIA office.)

"Haven't you been on the land, Mr. Fiddle?" asked the judge.

"No, Your Honor, but—"

"How do you know where the land is if you haven't seen it, Mr. Fiddle?" intoned Hodge.

"Well, it's all in the records, the act, land registry, the places I've looked to check title."

"But, without that stuff, you couldn't go up with me to Lake Louise and if I wanted to view the place, just show me where the Point Wrangell land is?"

"I'm afraid not, Judge Hodge."

"And yet you tell me you can tell me who owns land you ain't seen [the judge got colloquial when he got excited]."

"Yes, Your Honor," beamed Fiddle coming on strong.

"I'll be damned," said the judge in another remark the reporter missed. "Objection sustained. If he can't find the land, it is irrelevant who he says owns it. Maybe we've got the wrong defendants here. Maybe there ain't even any right defendants. Maybe it's just moose and wolves and bear you're after, Mr. Rodgers."

The judge was getting excited. He started to see a way out of this long trial (now well into the first day).

"Do you have a license to evict animals?" inquired the judge. A titter spread through the crowd.

"Your Honor, if I can go on, maybe we can get from Mr. Fiddle what the best evidence of title is, in his expert opinion, and then I'll develop that."

In the lawyers' row, murmurs indicated that maybe Rodgers did have a move or two in his lawyer's bag.

"Objection, Your Honor. If Mr. Fiddle isn't the best evidence of title, then he can't testify what the best evidence is."

"Sustained. Court's in recess for lunch."

Rodgers was relieved. His own suggestion about the best evidence to prove the government's case was turning out to be a fatal accident of an idea.

"What do we do, Trent?" Russell was a little irked by the *we*'s when it was trouble for Rodgers, but *I*'s when things went well.

"We can't do anything unless we prove who owns the land, and so far as I remember, it takes a deed to do that."

"Right," said expert Fiddle. "That's how you know who owns land."

"Where's the deed?" Trent asked.

"In Washington," said Fiddle.

"Damn," said Rodgers.

"But I have a certified copy," said Fiddle.

"Yes, but can you tell it's for the land where the Wrangell folks live?"

"No, I told this judge—"

"Who can?" asked Russell. "How do you know it's the right deed?"

"Because it refers to the coordinates of an aerial map."

"That's it. Use the certified copy of the deed, and have Doc Pierce verify the aerial map picture from the coordinates," said Russell in his finest contribution so far.

"Brilliant," said Rodgers. "I know just how to do it."

65

Russell left for a luncheon engagement, a three-shot whiskey one, at the Murmac. I left for a sandwich in my office, to find Judge Hodge getting his milk from my windowsill. It helped his ulcer. We reconvened at 1:30.

"Proceed, Mr. Rodgers."

"Your Honor, we want to offer a certified copy of the deed and—"

"How do you know it's the right deed?" asked Hodge.

"We'll tie it up, Your Honor."

"But Fiddle don't know Point Wrangell from Mount McKinley on a deed, Mr. Rodgers."

"Right, Your Honor, but Doc Pierce does, and the deed has coordinates, and the coordinates are linked to aerial maps, and I'm told Doctor Pierce, I don't know if he is an M.D. or not, but I'm told he knows the land and can verify the deed."

Croft was on his feet. He knew when to push and when to give. Letting the government use Doc Pierce, the best bush pilot out of Talkeetna, at least next to Don Shelden, couldn't help his case. Doc knew the country so damn well. He even knew the wolf families and where they lived. He had saved maybe a dozen lives with marvelous fly-ins. The "Doc" nickname came from three deliveries made while flying pregnant women to hospitals. He was a flying OB specialist without an M.D. degree, but an honorary Doctor because he was so well regarded. Frank was onto this.

"Doc," inquired Frank of the uneasy bush pilot, who was still sitting in the audience unsworn and who sure as hell didn't want to take the stand to help the BIA, "could you do what he says?"

"Yep," said the blushing Pierce.

"Stipulate to admitting the deed, Your Honor, on behalf of the Point Wrangell Baptists," said Frank.

"Accepted," said the judge.

"May the witness be excused?" asked Rodgers.

"Which witness?" asked the judge. "Fiddle, Pierce, or Croft?"

"Fiddle, Your Honor. He is the only one who is sworn and whose testimony counts."

"Do you reject the Croft stipulation as to what Doc Pierce would say?"

"Of course not, Your Honor."

"Should that testimony count as stipulated?"

"Yes, Your Honor."

"So Croft is OK, too?"

"Yes."

"That leaves Fiddle to be excused," said the judge.

"Your Honor, before we quit this, may I exercise my clients' God-given right to cross-examine Mr. Fiddle on his under-oath testimony?"

"Of course, Mr. Croft," said the judge.

"But, Your Honor," implored Reel Rodgers, "Fiddle has given no testimony that needs impeaching."

"Stipulate to that also," said Frank.

"Accepted by the court, Mr. Croft. Now Mr. Rodgers, are you telling me we've now used up almost a day on your case with your witness and there is 'no testimony'? For shame, Mr. Rodgers. Go to it, Frank."

"Thank you, Your Honor."

"Mr. Fiddle, sir, you have spent your entire adult life, peace and wartime, living off the largess of the U.S. of A., have you not?"

"I don't understand. What's largess, Mr. Croft?"

"You, in your adult life, have never been off the government payroll, have you?"

"No."

"Including today, and for testifying in this case?"

"Yes, sir."

"Including your wartime service in putting Japanese American farmers in concentration camps?"

"Objection," blurted Rodgers. "They weren't concentration camps."

"OK," said Frank. "Mr. Rodgers, the farmers were taken to the camps in military vehicles?"

"Yes."

"Under guard?"

"Yes."

"Put in stockades, that is, enclosures with wire fences around them?"

"Yes."

"With guards?"

"Yes."

"And held there, except the ones released to serve in the U.S. Army, for three to four years?"

"Yes."

"I'll accept the witness' description and withdraw my use of the term 'concentration camps.' "

"Thank you, Mr. Croft," said Judge Hodge. "Proceed."

"And you were paid, full pay, for that?"

"Yes."

"Any hazardous duty pay?" Frank was striking out with some no-lose-whatever-the-answer cross-examination questions.

"Not really. Only extra travel and per diem pay."

"So you could stay in hotels while you put the Japanese farmers in wired-in stockades?" Silence.

"Well? Well, you got the extra travel pay. Did you stay in the fancy hotels?"

"Not always."

"Where did you stay, with relatives?"

"No."

Frank knew he couldn't lose with this line.

"You stayed in officers' clubs, didn't you?"

"Yes," lamented Fiddle.

"Did you pay for that? Did you?"

"No."

"That's double-dipping, and in wartime," muttered Frank.

"Objection," came in Rodgers.

"What did Frank say?" asked the judge. "Read it back."

"That's double-dipping and in wartime," boomed Mable Wynot, the reporter, to make sure no one missed it.

"Frank, that double-dipping remark is out till argument. Go on."

"Thank you, Your Honor. Just two more questions, maybe three. How many millions of acres of land, which the government took from citizens, did you do the legal work for?"

"I don't know."

"It was in the millions, was it not?"

"Yes."

"Farmland, wasn't it?" inquired Frank.

"Yes."

"That's three, Frank."

"One more. May it please the court. *The important question.*"

"Go ahead, Mr. Croft," intoned the judge.

"And, Mr. Fiddle, the government took all those millions of acres of farmland from private citizens and did not pay them one penny for it, and then sold it to big-time business operators for a profit, did it not, sir?"

"Yes," quavered Fiddle.

"You are excused, for now," said Judge Hodge, who then inquired, "Who is your next witness, Mr. Rodgers?"

"Thumper Johnson, Your Honor. We call him as an adverse witness."

Thumper, looking genuinely uncomfortable, subpoena clutched in hand, came forward to be sworn. After reading the oath, hand held high, Thumper got on the witness stand and gave his name and locale. Before Rodgers could ask even question one, Croft inquired, "Can I *voir-dire* the witness, may it please the court?"

"Why?" "Why?" asked both the judge and Rodgers. "Can't say," said Frank. "My reasons are my work product."

"All right," said the judge. "I'll rule on the appropriateness when the questions are objected to."

"Fine, Your Honor."

"Captain Johnson, if you please, sir." (Thumper beamed at that). "You were subpoenaed by the BIA to testify here, were you not?"

"Yes, sir."

Frank Croft, Thumper Johnson, Judge Hodge

"Captain Johnson, do you bear the United States of America any ill will?"

"I do not, Mr. Croft."

"Do you know, Captain, sir, that the government has declared you to be adverse to them?"

"What does that mean, Lawyer Croft?"

"That you are against them: hostile, unfriendly, even enemylike."

"Well, I'll be damned," said Thumper.

"Now, Captain Johnson, you've been sworn here?"

"Yes."

"To tell the truth?"

"Yes."

"And will you tell the truth?"

"Yes, so help me God."

"Do you know why your telling the truth should make the government regard you as hostile?"

"I do not."

"Do you know why the government should be averse to having witnesses tell the truth?"

"I do not."

"Well, I want you to know, Captain Johnson, that the Point Wrangell Christian Baptists are in no way adverse or unfriendly because you took God's oath to tell the truth."

"I'm delighted and pleased, Lawyer Croft."

"The Wrangell Baptists regard you as their friend." Thirty-six amens were murmured in rows 1 though 6. "That's all I have, may it please the court" concluded Frank, relinquishing the witness.

"Please proceed, Mr. Rodgers, with your hostile questioning," said the judge.

Thumper Johnson was relieved and a little fired up. He had started the whole shebang by ratting on the Wrangell Baptists. Since then, he had often felt that even for a man who lived from rash moment to rash moment that his act had been "goddamn foolish" because it made him out to be an ally, even a friend, of the BIA. Worse still, it had looked as if he would have to testify in court *for* the BIA.

Plainly, Alaska sentiment would be against him, from the Anchorage Christian community to the Nome natives to the bushmen. It was the latter group that Thumper was most concerned with. Like him, they lived "out there," beyond the boundaries of day-to-day in-town legal conduct or city morality. In the bush, men did what was right, however wrong anyone else thought it was. Turning people in, aiding the government, not sharing, were sins in the wilderness. The bushers could punish sinners in their own way, as Thumper well knew.

Frank Croft with his *voir dire* had changed all that. Frank had pointed out that Thumper remained a friend of the Baptists, and more importantly that he was a foe of the BIA. Thumper was spoiling for a fight as Rodgers began his questioning.

"Where do you live, Mr. Johnson?"

"When?" said Thumper.

"Today," said Rodgers.

"At the Cook Arms Apartments, N Street, Anchorage."

"For how long?" inquired a surprised Rodgers.

"Two nights, so far."

"Oh, I see, I apologize. I really meant to ask, Where did you live in 1961?" stated Rodgers.

"Oh," said Thumper.

"Where did you live in 1961?" inquired an exasperated Rodgers.

"When?" asked Thumper.

"In the fall of 1961?"

"I don't remember" said Johnson.

"Mr. Johnson, didn't you live on Lake Louise, Alaska?"

"At or on, Mr. Rodgers?"

"What is the difference?"

"Don't you know, Mr. Rodgers?"

"No, I don't, Captain."

"Oh," said Thumper again.

Back in the lawyers' row during the ensuing pause, Wendell Kay could be heard to observe, "This could be a long afternoon."

Rodgers, now as flustered in his cross-exam as he had been pleased with his direct exam of Fiddle, was floundering. A note from Straub got him back on track. Reading it aloud to Thumper, he got back to where Captain Johnson had derailed him.

"What is the difference between living at or on Lake Louise?"

"Mr. Rodgers, you can only live on a lake in winter; in summer, you live on a boat in the lake, or at a lake if you ain't on a boat."

This kind of semantic sparring as to Thumper's 1961 whereabouts went on for another ten minutes, when Rodgers had the belated sense to switch his approach and use leading questions.

"Mr. Johnson—"

"Captain, if you please," injected Thumper.

"Captain Johnson, did you see a settlement of human beings on land on Point Wrangell in the Lake Louise area on or about September 17, 1961?"

Thumper, reluctantly: "Yes."

"Was the area in which you saw them known to you to be United States government-owned land?"

"So I've been led to believe."

"Do you recognize any of those people as now being in this courtroom?"

"Hard to tell. Maybe."

"Who?"

Again reluctantly: "The Reverend Doheney."

"What did you do after you saw the settlers at Point Wrangell?"

"I went home."

"Did you, Mr.—Captain Johnson, at any time after seeing the Wrangell Christians, report to Mr. Fiddle at the BIA office about the people you saw and where you saw them?"

"Probably."

"*Why* did you do that, Captain?" inquired Rodgers charging ahead.

("I was afraid he wouldn't ask," said Bailey Sanders to John Manders.)

"Because I was hung over and—"

"What did you tell Mr. Fiddle?" cut in Rodgers.

"Objection, Your Honor, Captain Johnson has not completed his answer."

"Sustained," said Judge Hodge. "Proceed, Thumper, with telling us why you went to Fiddle."

"I will, Your Honor, and Mr. Croft. You see, when I'm hung over, I don't think so good. The goodness I develop in me when I'm drunk turns sour real bad. I don't think right. I get kind of deluded. And I had delusions of hangover when I thought Fiddle and the BIA had any business interrupting the God-directed activities of these nice Baptists."

"Objection, Your Honor, this is irrelevant to the facts."

"Mr. Rodgers, you asked him 'Why?' and the government has a right to a truthful response to its questions. Go on, Captain."

Thumper started to warm to his task. "These good Baptists seemed divinely brought to that lonely but beautiful spot. It was some Devil-inspired thing that sent me to the feds. I saw them living a good wholesome life there, trying to make homes in that tough country. The women worked so hard, and were so nice and good, and the little kids brightened up the wilderness. I know in my heart, now, it was wrong to have turned them in. I Pray to God I'll be forgiven for it."

There were more amens from the pews.

Stumble and Fall were reeling at the counsel table, but Rodgers, with the poor lawyer's instinct for making a bad witness even worse, went on.

"You did see the Baptists there on the government land, did you not?" Rodgers was fixated on that, because even the government couldn't evict if it couldn't locate.

"Now that you ask again, Mr. Rodgers, and because I really want to tell the truth for you, I got to say I ain't sure. I could have been hallucinating. When I'm hung over, things seem different than I thought they was. Why, sometimes I've woken up in the morning with a hangover with an older lady, when the night before I was sure I went to bed with a beautiful young woman. Mr. Rodgers, you got me mixed up now, I ain't sure what I recall."

"Court's in recess for the day," ordered Judge Hodge. "We'll be in session again starting next Tuesday."

"Tuesday?" asked Rodgers. "Why, that means we'll be held over well into next week, with Thursday and Friday still available this week. Why?"

"Mr. Rodgers, I thought you had asked enough 'why' questions already today. This case ain't going to stop all justice in Alaska even if you want it to. I have motions to hear, pleas to consider, rulings to make, and I will. Tuesday we'll reconvene."

"May it please the court?"

"Yes, Mr. Croft?"

"Well, I'm reluctant to ask, Your Honor, but how do subpoenaed witnesses like Captain Johnson, here because of the BIA case, get by for funds to stay here in town?"

"Thank you, Mr. Croft, you are right. All subpoenaed witnesses are held over at the same per diem as the government lawyers get. That's only right, isn't it, Mr. Rodgers?"

A reluctant "yes" from Rodgers, who would have fainted on the spot if he had known that Frank had subpoenaed thirty-six Baptists as well as six bushmen as potential witnesses.

"Could I ask Mr. Rodgers how much that is per diem, Your Honor?"

"Certainly, Mr. Croft."

"What is your per diem, Mr. Rodgers?"

"Seventy dollars a day" was the reply.

"Seventy dollars? Seems like a lot," the judge noted.

"Well, we get extra here in Alaska, Your Honor."

"Seventy dollars every day in advance?"

"Yes, Your Honor, we have to pay hotels, food, et cetera."

"Seems fair," said Frank. "Your Honor, could the subpoenaed witnesses get theirs in advance, too?"

"Seems fair," said Hodge. "Work it out, Mr Rodgers, will you?"

"Yes, Your Honor. Are there more witnesses than the Captain?"

"Yup," said Frank, "forty-two, and at $70 a day that's $2,940 a day. For the eight days so far, and a couple more in advance toward Tuesday's, that's $29,400," said Frank in one of the quickest calculations he'd ever done.

"We are in recess," finalized Hodge.

The courtroom was a real hummer of activity. Smiles were everywhere. Frank had just gotten one of the bigger awards in Alaska in months. His side of the case hadn't even started, and his clients were the defendants. Bailey Sanders and John Manders were over congratulating him.

"Some of the best lawyering of my time," said old John. "George Grigsby [the legendary Dean of the Alaska Bar] couldn't have done better."

"Thanks," said Frank, "I'll buy drinks for the Association," knowing what was an appropriate rejoinder.

"Praise the Lord for his bounty to us," announced Reverend Doheney to his pack.

Thumper and the six lucky subpoenaed bushmen left with the prospect of more real dollars in hand than they would get from a whole season of swishing around a miner's pan for flecks of gold.

The Washington legal trinity was aghast. This lead-pipe-cinch case was going to cost more to try than if they had conceded that the land was owned by the Baptists and then taken it by right of eminent domain. "Up that way," as Russell pointed out, "forty acres, if it's real good, with gold prospects, you might get for a thousand dollars, more like five or six hundred, about twelve-fifty or fifteen an acre."

Feldstein said, "For $29,400 we could have got twelve hundred acres, maybe twenty-four hundred."

"Yes," said Russell.

"Keep quiet," said Rodgers.

Well, the weekend strategy meetings weren't all that much fun. Even by BIA standards, this case wasn't proceeding "too good." Up to this point, win or lose, the government had spent maybe ten to twelve times what the land could have been bought for if they didn't own it. But, as Fiddle explained, "When it comes to defending the taxpayer's monies as we must, it does not matter how much we spend, it is the principle that counts."

That lofty principle idea wasn't picked up too much when we read "Write" Wright's weekend report on the trial. "Key Government Witness Turns State's Evidence" began the story.

In a dramatic courtroom testimony, Captain Thumper Johnson conceded to his own lawyer, Attorney Rodgers of the BIA, that he wasn't sure if he had ever seen the defendants on the land the Government says it owns. "If they aren't there they'll be hard to evict," according to local bar leaders Sanders and Manders. [Frank's "drinks on the house" weekend was starting to pay off.]

Wright had gone on to do a nice job of describing the Baptists as God-directed people living in a hard world. In the final part of the article and "because it is of interest to my national audience," he wrote:

The BIA seems willing to pay anything for justice. While this reporter can't find out what the five lawyers working on this case are paid, [George and I raised hell on that one for we wanted no part of the glory of the government victory. "Write" said he'd take care of us later; it was just that he was totally committed to a reporter's accuracy] we have learned that the government's daily per diem payments for the trial now exceed $4,000 a day, a record by Alaskan standards.

Write didn't bother to tell that there were thirty-six Baptist and six bushman witnesses sharing in the per diem payments, for he felt national audiences didn't go much for such local matters. Later, when Senator Gruening saw the story in the Washington Post, he demanded an audit of the BIA. It kind of tailed off when the senator found out it was his constituents who got most of the money.

The big legal problem left for the BIA was to get some people on the land to evict. Rodgers had undercut Thumper's testimony enough that the government's case was in doubt. Feldstein made the suggestion that they finally decided to go with: "Call the Reverend. He guided his pack there. He'll admit it."

During the weekend recess, when word got out about the $70 per day for subpoenaed witnesses, Frank was deluged with people offering to testify who saw the Baptists there or didn't—"it all depends, Frank, on what the truth should be." One miner who had drifted down from Ester City, a small place some two hundred miles from Lake Louise, was quite sure he had seen the Baptists "right near Fairbanks when I was hung over." Frank thanked them all but, being a responsible lawyer, didn't want to overreach for his client's cause, particularly now that he was assured of a fee from the thirty-six Baptists' $70 per diems.

Tuesday dawned at about 12:07 A.M., as it was June in Anchorage. Being as it was day all night, Captain Johnson and his fans had not wasted a lot of their per diem on lodging. Thumper, assisted and supported by his six wealthy bushman friends, again made it to the courthouse.

" 'Hangover' don't describe Thumper yet," Russell observed to me. "He's still in the good-drunk stage 'cause he ain't off his high yet. On good booze Thumper can stay up for days."

Thumper was primed for the witness stand. Instead of being an "enemy of the people" as a government adverse witness, he had turned out to be the people's friend because of the people's lawyer, Frank Croft. Through the subpoena's power he had brought a small economic boom to the Bush economy. And on Tuesday, he was even more unsure of whether he had ever seen any "Christians" at Lake Louise.

Thumper kind of hallucinated to the witness stand and, as court was called, announced to the judge: "I'm ready to tell the truth, Your Honor."

"Fine," said the judge. "Did you have a good weekend?"

"Wonderful, Your Honor, and would you like to ask me why?"

"I would," said the judge, "but that's for the lawyers. Mr. Rodgers, proceed."

"No questions, Your Honor."

"Mr. Croft?"

"No questions, Your Honor. The Defense rests."

"Rests?!" exclaimed Rodgers. "You can't."

"Why can't they?" asked Hodge. Even Rodgers knew the answer to this one: "Because the government's case isn't over yet. We're going to call the Reverend Doheney."

"All right," said Hodge. "What about that, Mr. Croft?"

"Well, it seems unfair to use our witness to prove his case. We'd like to go over until tomorrow because my good Christian clients were ready to rest our case. Now that their leader is being called, I want to see if he should take the Fifth Amendment or the Fourteenth Amendment or whatever."

"Seems reasonable," said the judge, "with this new turn of events."

"The government objects, Your Honor. This is preposterous. Mr. Croft knows there is no Fifth Amendment claim in a civil case, and there is no Fourteenth Amendment claim here. All we are doing is—"

"Taking people's property," the judge testily objected. "Without paying. And under a statute you didn't read enough to know that there wouldn't be a jury trial, causing a lot of Alaskans considerable interruption in their daily lives—as well as lost income. Mr. Rodgers, you surely won't mind if Lawyer Croft does just check a little, like overnight, on his clients' constitutional rights. As a matter of fact, the BIA lawyers might look at the Constitution too—that is the United States Constitution, Mr. Rodgers. If the BIA doesn't have a copy, I'll loan them one, if Mr. Croft doesn't mind."

"They can have a copy of mine," Frank graciously offered.

Rodgers, despite the castigation, just didn't know when to quit.

"Well, then, Your Honor," he began petulantly, "can the thirty-six subpoenaed witnesses at least be released?"

"What about it, Frank?"

"No, Your Honor. Now that we can't rest, I just don't know what might come up. We might need them all. Of course, the Reverend himself gets no fee as a party, but for the others—"

"OK," said Hodge. "Advance another day's per diem to the witnesses, Marshal Coleburn. Court will reconvene at 10 A.M. tomorrow."

THE PROMISED LAND

The hard part of the case for the Baptists had come. The hard part of most cases comes when your own client has to testify. The Reverend Doheney would be the principal witness for his own cause—and maybe against it.

As the members of the Murmac Bar Association all knew, "there is nothing like your own witness to screw up a case." A witness who had sold land in California, and who could sell religion in Alaska, had the potential to be a disaster. On top of all that, the trial so far and the judge's rather discernible leaning for the Alaskan zealots had the Reverend righteously fired up.

Frank Croft did his best to cool the Reverend down. He gave the usual instructions: "Listen to the questions," "Don't answer if you don't really *know* the answer," and, above all, "Keep the answers short, don't volunteer nothing."

"Right," said the Reverend Doheney very righteously.

"The People call the Reverend Doheney," announced Rodgers. He had picked up that part about "representing the People" from discussions with Russell and me. Frank wasn't going to let it slide by.

"What 'People' called the Reverend?" inquired Frank. And, answering his own question, "He's called by the damned BIA."

"Order," said the judge as the Reverend came forward to be sworn, his own Bible in hand.

The Reverend sure looked the part: tall, gaunt, black beard flecked with gray, more hair on his face than on his head. Part of his face was red from exposure to the elements. His brow, protected by a cap, was as white as his clerical collar. He wore old mukluks, black wool trousers, and a red-and-black-plaid wool shirt with a clerical collar insert of black and white. He was a spangle of checks, with vertical white lines at collar and crown.

"Do you swear to tell the truth, the whole truth, and nothing but the truth?" intoned the marshal.

"By Almighty God, our Christian Father, Who has led us into this wilderness, I do." ("He is making the closing argument," whispered Manders to Bailey.)

"I object," said Rodgers. The judge looked amazed and aggrieved. "You are objecting to your witness taking the oath, Mr. Rodgers?"

"Not that, Your Honor, but he is making a speech."

"Mr. Rodgers," said Hodge, "the man is giving his Christian oath. You ain't against religious freedom, are you? Is that the government's idea in this case for a defense?"

"No, Your Honor, but—"

"Go on, Reverend."

"Thank you, Your Honor. As I was saying: By Almighty God, our good and Christian Father, Who has led our small pack to this great land and settled us in homes by clear waters—by that Almighty and Righteous God, I will tell the complete truth."

Rodgers: "Is your Baptist colony, all thirty-six of you, settled on the waters along Lake Louise as shown in this picture, Exhibit A, at map coordinates North sixty-two degrees, seventeen minutes, West one hundred and forty-six degrees, twenty-eight minutes?"

"By Almighty God, we are, Mr. Rodgers."

"He's just lost the damned case," whispered Manders to Bailey, "because of the enthusiasm of his religious veracity."

"Don't be too sure," said Bailey. "Rodgers ain't through yet."

And of course, he wasn't. Being at that point where he had asked the right questions and got the right answers, Rodgers could no more quit than Thumper could drink one whiskey. He was addicted to bad lawyering.

"Who are the members of your congregation?"

"All God's people."

"Who are the members who are settled at Lake Louise?"

"Well, there are the elders Waisanek from Poland, who came in the Depression to Matanuska, and who are now supported by our pack. There is Mr. and Mrs. Elmo Johnson; their two sons, Jon, aged nine, and Leroy, eleven; and . . . ."

The Reverend took the next twenty minutes filling the courtroom with the personalities and background of each member of his pack. It was an impressively loving display. Even Rodgers seemed sucked into it, and, as the Reverend paused, he asked, "What did your congregation do there?"

Reverend Doheney slid right into a solid second gear: "We worship the Lord through our prayers and our work and in our daily lives. We have plowed his earth . . . to feed ourselves . . . we have . . . ."

And now came the Reverend's story of the domesticating of that wilderness, of the hardship of homesteading, of men and women working the wilderness, of good people, Christian families, young and old working together for God. When the Reverend eased up on that, there wasn't a dry eye in the house. Amens were coming strong, even from the bushmen. Some thought Thumper Johnson was humming a hymn in the background, but those closest to him saw that he had dozed off. God and whiskey always made Thumper sleepy. The Reverend was still warming to it. Rodgers, driven to botch things up, made this inevitable. "Why did you settle there with your pack?"

The Promised Land

The Reverend went right into high gear, his white brow glistening with beads of sweat, his Adam's apple bumping on the white clerical collar, his voice like a Chinook wind, coming warm and soft through a snow-covered forest.

"God told us to," and in a lowered voice, "He talked to me—in the Redwoods of California, near Eureka. He said He would lead us from trouble to a good land . . . and direct us there. We assembled our resources and . . . ."

It turned into a religious travelogue, a saga of people struggling up the gravel trail of the Alcan Highway. A few converts here, another two or three additions there, then joining up with the Detroit group. Finally, the addition of the older Polish folk, all traveling together until they got to Lake Louise.

Reverend Doheney was giving the sermon of his life.

"We came to Lake Louise, tired, hungry, still searching, when the setting sun of an August day . . . framed before us an unusual tree, Alaska spruce, shaped like a cross . . . before the low rays of the summer sun. As I saw it . . . God again spoke to me, inside me. 'This is the place; you have arrived. Care for your pack, as I direct.' "

Well, the courtroom was quiet—"Quiet quiet," as Joe Slade described it. Not a word; even Judge Hodge seemed out of control.

Frank Croft was confused. He knew his client had just blown the case, but it felt like a win. He didn't know what to do. To ask the Reverend a question would be to carry snow to Nome. To present nothing seemed to leave the government with a sure win, for the Reverend had righteously, but accurately, placed his flock just where the government could evict them.

Hodge saved the day.

"Court's in recess until Thursday." Even Rodgers didn't ask Hodge why he wanted an extra day, or about expense advances.

There was a strange feeling to the situation. Frank's case seemed a sure loser, but the day didn't leave him feeling too bad. The government had a sure winner, but the day's outcome didn't leave us feeling too good, at least Russell and me. A win for the BIA wouldn't do much for our Alaska reputations.

The Washington lawyers started to get their real characters back. They were, after all, BIA lawyers. Evicting decent people was routine work. Winning was what counted for the bureaucracy. Justice had little to do with that.

"This case will make you legal chief of the bureau," said Feldstein to Rodgers. "A trial, contested in a *foreign* [Russell and I heard that, all right] court."

"Great examination," said Straub, "and that ending, with Doheney. Lawyer Croft's own witness did him in. The judge is stuck. Even if he rules against us, the record is solid. We'll take his ass in the court of appeals. All it will take is time and money."

"And keep more BIA-tax paid lawyers employed," whispered Trent to me.

On Wednesday, I knew the judge was up to something. Law books were being brought to his chambers, even the annotated United States Codes with the small print. Marshal Coleburn was in and out with aerials and maps. I kept quiet about this, except to report to Rodgers when he asked what was going on: "The judge may be planning a fishing trip," which he could have been, although I didn't think he was.

Thursday dawned, unusually fine for an Anchorage June. In fact, it was the day of the summer solstice. It would be the longest day of the year. And a long, sunny summer day in Alaska is the best day of the year. Mount McKinley, dancing on the horizon two hundred miles away, looked telephoto close. It made you know why natives had named Denali "majestic mountain" and considered it a religious place. There was something spiritual in the air about the day. The courthouse was jammed. Everyone seemed to know something special would happen. No one knew what.

The Reverend was in the witness chair. Frank, duly counseled by all the wisdom of the Murmac Bar Association lawyers, both drunk and sober, had made his decision. He had made it in a time honored way. Cold sober, he evaluated the case and made up his mind what was right. Then he got drunk, deliberately and pleasantly with Bailey and John. They reviewed the case once again, and, while drunk, he again made a decision: the same one. As Frank observed, "Anytime I make the same decision, both sober and drunk, it's as good a decision as I can get to."

So, with the Reverend back on the stand, Frank got up and said, "No questions, Your Honor, the defense rests."

"Wait a minute, Mr. Croft," the judge said. "Before you rest, I got some questions."

"Proceed, Your Honor," said Croft.

Judge Hodge began: "You do believe in the United States of America, do you not Reverend?"

"I do, Your Honor."

"You do believe that we are a Christian and God-conceived country under its Constitution?"

"Yes, Your Honor."

"Do you understand, Reverend, that we judges are sworn, in my case on a Bible like yours, to uphold the Constitution?"

"Yes, I do."

"So you do believe in our courts and their God-given powers?"

"I do, my people do."

"I'm glad of that, Reverend, for in pondering this case, God came to me in my deliberations. I needed divine guidance. He instructed me, Reverend, that you and your pack weren't in the right place."

A murmur in the courtroom. The Reverend looked surprised. "Oh, it was all right for two years for spiritual training and conditioning, but now, with a new season starting, there is a new place for you and your congregation. Forty-acre sites for every family. If you just work them for two years and build homes there, they become yours, and these places are located at . . . ."

Well, the judge had spent hours and days with the marshal digging out the best homestead sites still available. They happened to be right in the spot God spoke to the judge about. To me, God's other instructions to Hodge sounded very much like the legal requirements to establish a homestead (as Russell said, "God probably knows the law."). It was an act of judicial genius, kind of a miracle.

"Of course, Mr. Rodgers, there will be costs associated with moving the Baptists, so I'll be assessing travel charges against the government to relocate all of these people and their belongings. I'm sure Mr. Croft and Mr. Trent can work that out."

"Trent?" inquired Rodgers.

"Yes, Mr. Rodgers, I want Alaska's United States Attorney Trent to handle the government cost matters here. Travel charges will be an Alaska-incurred expense. While you've done a fine job in my court, I can't give you a general license to practice here. The costs are to come from the BIA budget, because we don't want to otherwise limit the general good work of the United States attorney here in Alaska.

"Will you accept that responsibility, Mr. Trent?"

"Willingly, Your Honor," said Russell who aspired to political office in Alaska. He knew that being able to put federal monies in the hands of Alaska citizens would not hurt that.

"Will you accept my God-directed rulings, Reverend?"

"I will, we will," said the Reverend, knowing very well when a good real estate deal had been made.

"And, Mr. Croft, you did a fine job—even if your clients will have to move."

"Thank you, Your Honor, and we accept your ruling. It's just the way of it for a trial lawyer. You win some, you lose some."

• • •

How do I come to remember such episodes? It is a trial lawyer's trick, picking selected facts, remembering warm anecdotes from interesting raconteurs, unblemished in the main by facts.

With that warning, let me tell you how it all happened.

Trial
Number
One

My mind preserves it as if the whole adventure happened yesterday. It was my first trial. The setting: Worcester, Massachusetts, the heart of the Commonwealth. The time: October, 1957. I was a lawyer. My license said so. And lawyers went to court and tried cases. My instructing counselor was W. Hurlbert Rice: New England Yankee to his McIntosh-Apple core. He was then in his eighty-fifth year, diminutive in size, but of formidable stature in the Massachusetts legal community and a giant at the probate bar in Worcester County.

At eighty-four, Mr. Rice twinkled. He was old line Yankee but had missed that dominant gene of his peers, taciturn dourness. Mr. Rice spoke quietly, his advice laced with humor and pertinence. The Massachusetts legal system of the fifties seemed linked to its British heritage of a divided bar: solicitors, who do not go to court but who prepare cases, facts, and law to instruct their trial brethren, as distinguished from the barristers, that far smaller group of trial advocates who alone have access to the high courts. Whatever the reason, W. Hurlbert Rice, Esquire, enjoyed the role of a solicitor and was renowned for his sage counsel. People wanted Mr. Rice's advice and, even more unusual to the human condition, wanted to follow it. The trial arena he left for those he could instruct on the law and facts.

Hurlbert and I had common bonds. Our ancestors had arrived by ships on the Massachusetts shores and then moved on to Worcester. His, I think, came on the *Mayflower*, mine had just landed. There was another bond, perhaps more special. We were both graduates of Dartmouth College. Mr. Rice graduated in the Class of 1892 some 60 years before me. Our common experience of boyhood learning at a small college, where change comes slowly in buildings and professors and not at all in the New Hampshire weather and character of its inhabitants, gave us much to discuss. I had been a skiing competitor, jumping and cross-country. It was a mystery to W. Hurlbert how anyone could enjoy such escapades out of doors in winter. That was the time when his fine mind had turned to classics, especially the reading of Latin. Latin was, even to the 1950s, an intrinsic part of most legal education, and mastery of it added to his legal stature.

Mr. Rice fostered in me a lifelong concern for the written word—what it tells and what it reveals about people: "Watch what the jurors are reading, which books and newspapers. Find out if they don't read and why. Are they poor, dumb, immigrants, lazy or neglected? Learning a juror's attitude toward information will tell you more about that person than a thousand questions will yield.

"And you—you read the newspapers for the local news and views. This will be a sign of what the jurors and judges care about. Issues of local notoriety, politicians, deaths, business, and the sensations of the day sell papers because people want to read about them. What people read forms their views. It is no accident that conservative voters read conservative papers. With that background, you'll know how to best tell your client's story so a jury will want to believe it."

That is sound advice to this day, subject only to the caveat that the spread of TV imagery and radio may make the reading juror more significant. But it is even more important to know how all the jurors receive their daily dose of information about the world outside the courtroom.

In one of the honored traditions of his time, Mr. Rice had not gone to law school. He had officed with some venerable of the Massachusetts bar whose name fades. Was it George Hoar, or Arthur Rugg, or only Francis Gaskill? Whoever his tutor, Mr. Rice had long been described by Frank Smith as "the firm's lawyer" and Frank for years had made the rain for Thayer, Smith & Gaskill. Legal scholar always, and possessed of a remarkable terseness, Hurlbert had literally surrounded himself with every letter, brief, contract, will, or trust he had written. Each word was handsomely letterpressed on onionskin paper and leatherbound for his office bookshelves. Bearing the responsibility of living in the same room with all his writings, Hurlbert used his words well. He might at any time turn to them, very much as if they were recalled from an ancient computer: what he had written to Bill Parson in 1917, or what Clarence Swain's trust provided in 1911.

Hurlbert's domain was protected by Patience Seymour, maiden secretary par excellence. Her name well suited her New England heritage. Miss Seymour came into this world mature. She had aquiline, Yankee features set off by clear, gray eyes. Born in a rural Massachusetts town, as the oldest child she had to leave the loving confines of a large family to go to work to help the many sisters and brothers still at home. Miss Seymour had quickly worked her way up to become secretary of *the* senior partner. And even as Hurlbert was a partner with lawyers, Miss Seymour was a partner with Mr. Rice.

Together they ushered the history of the firm slowly forward. Each accepted progress, but at a temperate pace that they trusted. Thus, while typewriters and carbon paper and copy machines were fine for an "up-to-date law firm," the firm's having such devices did not mean that he and Miss Seymour need employ them. Indeed, Miss Seymour, in starched dresses, spring-fresh whatever the season, and Hurlbert, bow tie brightening his three-piece suits, would have appeared out of place tangling with modern mechanisms. Together they acquiesced to change while clinging to their own precedents.

With Mr. Rice's support, Patience had disdained carbon paper as some innovative nonsense. All of Hurlbert's written words were daily letterpressed. Patience spinning down the clamping mechanism of the letterpress, would squeeze the typed-page words to onionskin pages, all to be bound in handsome leather volumes. The transferring agent was a moist, prepared paper, which left a parchment feel to the original page when it dried and gave an immediate odor of musty antiquity to the leather-encased onionskin copies.

On an August afternoon, only days after I came to the firm, Mr. Rice, at the behest of Miss Seymour, called me into his moistly fragrant chamber. "Young Lawyer Lundquist," the diminutive giant intoned, "Miss Seymour's neighbor, Sara Appleton, has to go to court, and it's a job for you to do. A new neighbor who bought the house next door is gardening Mrs. Appleton out of a yard. You'll have to stop it in court."

Miss Seymour summed up the problem: "A new mover-inner, an Italian man, has purchased the property uphill to Sara Appleton." He was gardening it in good Italian fashion; but when it rained, water channeled through rows of lettuce and tomatoes and funneled onto Mrs. Appleton's land. With abundant New England afternoon thundershowers, her lawn became soggy and her back sidewalk awash. Mrs. Appleton's temper and temperament became charged with lightning sound and thunderous fury.

I wanted to visit with Mrs. Appleton to get the facts, but Miss Seymour, with her many years in the law with Mr. Rice, assured me it wasn't necessary. She would assist (read "instruct") me. Under Miss Seymour's tutelage, a complaint was

quickly drawn from a model found midst Mr. Rice's onionskin trove. Miss Seymour assured me that equity could stop
the flood and that law would permit a damage award for the
diminished value of the Appleton property. This lawyer work
would mollify and compensate the widow. It would "probably all be accomplished just with filing a complaint." I was
only to be involved "in case it doesn't work, and it has to
go to a court trial." While that theme, "filing the complaint
will do it," has played to different facts and, perchance, larger
issues for much of the rest of my life, it was for me the first
beckoning of the client's siren song to the lawyer: "Just file
a complaint and we'll get results!" This faith in lawyer's
magic is usually followed by a mandate to "get enough in
damages to make your efforts worthwhile."

That first claim was for $250. As I reflect back, the biggest
change in all these years has been in adding ciphers to the
dollar figure claimed. So the law progresses. We reckoned
without the awareness of Mr. Giovannini, Appleton's neighbor. He knew, as did every good Italian resident of Worcester,
that when law entered the picture so did Banducci and Banducci, gifted brothers enriched by and famous for their success at law—Nicholas for out-of-court matters and Buzzy for
trials. So great was their tie to the Italian community that
they owned that ethnic practice.

It was not just ethnic links that drew clients to the Banduccis and especially to Buzzy. In the courtroom, Mr. Banducci got results. Wherever the appellation "Buzzy" came
from, it had nothing to do with voice or physique. He spoke
in the quiet, yet precise and almost reverent tones of an
undertaker. Like many a good plaintiff's lawyer, he had a
gift for the soft voice that drew ears to listen, rather than the
bombastic eloquence that turns them away.

The drawing voice and elegant presence were all the
more devastating because of Mr. Banducci's superlative
mastery of the tricks of his trade. In that prediscovery era
there was little chance to assess the opponent's case. Legal
wiliness was a craft. Mr. Banducci's talent was to produce

surprise witnesses: off duty police officers who observed the accident, doctors who diagnosed injuries unusual to the human condition, and attractive, grieving widows with child in arms. Mr. Banducci's well cast witnesses became living demonstrative evidence before that term had been coined. They were even more effective because from the witness stand they played out for the jury their scripted roles. Each was a clearly defined character in the soap opera of ordinary people that plays daily in the courtrooms of our land.

Whatever their prosperity, the Banduccis had not outgrown their neighborhood. They lived in a three-decker flat in the Shrewsbury Street neighborhood of Worcester, while they officed at a fine building downtown. But wherever they officed, the Banduccis practiced law everywhere and all the time.

In an era when "ambulance chasing" was more than a derogatory comment (it was a crime), to avoid chasing, a successful but aspiring immigrant lawyer had to be everywhere, attend everything, and, if possible, support all causes. There was therefore not a wake or a wedding missed by the Banducci brothers, or an Italian lodge or baseball team that did not enjoy their support. In turn, the entire Italian community became their clients. A fond anecdote of the time was that one Banducci problem arose when after a bus-truck accident, the number of his passenger plaintiffs who filed suit exceeded the capacity of the bus.

Court congestion in Worcester existed because "How many courts can I be in at one time, Your Honor?" had been for years a standard Buzzy Banducci continuance request. This legal logjam had been broken, however, by Judge John Delancey of the Worcester County Supreme Judicial Bench who, upon observing the County's tumescent trial calendar, had replied to Buzzy Banducci with a forthright judicial answer: "In all of them where your firm's name is called, Mr. Banducci—starting ninety days forward—or there will be defaults if there is no one to try the case."

Buzzy Banducci considered tempting fate by clinging personally to each client's cause. He permitted discretion to overcome legal valor or ego, however, and started a law firm when he learned that Judge Delancey had defaulted a Boston lawyer's client on a long-trailing case because the lawyer was in the men's room when the case was called. So the Banduccis added lawyers to their office.

While our filing the complaint had not caused Mr. Giovannini to "give up," at least (Miss Seymour reported) I wouldn't have to "deal with Buzzy Banducci, Esquire, himself in my first trial." A trial of this nature would most certainly be turned over to one of his minions. For that, at least, I was grateful. To get ready for trial I needed to meet Mrs. Appleton. But Miss Seymour assured me that the day before trial would allow plenty of time: "There is no sense getting ready more than once, as the trial may be continued. We have good evidence, pictures and all."

From the Banducci office on behalf of Mr. Giovannini, we received only a general denial and a jury demand. Miss Seymour was uncertain about the jury. She favored judges, both for equity and the modest damages that, as a good Yankee, she thought would be appropriate; but on the other hand, we were the plaintiff. (Miss Seymour had a basic distrust of plaintiffs common to those who do most of their law work for the defense.)

"A jury could be good for us," she said, "but they shouldn't give Sara too much money. She doesn't need it. It's all up to you, Weyman." I thought of consulting Miss Seymour as to how the jury might be held in check in my search for $250 worth of justice, but decided that this was one trial risk I'd accept for myself.

I didn't know who from the newly expanded Banducci chambers would be assigned this plum of a case, and I wouldn't find out until the day of the trial. Neither party was about to fiddle with pretrial matters. The judge would sort out law, equity, and even the need for a jury when we got there, advised Patience.

The only permissible discovery in Massachusetts, absent something as desperate as a dying witness, was interrogatories (questions to the other party to be answered under oath), twenty in number. Because lawyer tradition called for most of these to be used up by requests for what we already knew (name, address, age, place of birth, marital status, occupation, and religion), interrogatories weren't much help. Any direct question about the case would produce "only lawyer's words," said Miss Seymour. On her advice, I decided to forgo their use.

In return, Miss Seymour permitted my billable pretrial preparation time with the Widow Appleton to be expanded to a full two hours on the day before trial. Miss Seymour would not permit a nonchargeable encounter, not at $12.50 an hour for lawyers' time. "It would start a bad habit," she pronounced, reminding me of what President Lincoln said about "a lawyer's time being his stock in trade." Miss Seymour spoke as if she had met that great advocate president personally; more likely, her mother met him.

The afternoon arrived. Miss Seymour chose not to expose Mrs. Appleton's client confidences to others who officed with me in the firm's small library. She had informed herself about which lawyers were away that day. Bob Bowditch, one of the firm's most significant partners, was among them; so I got to use his large office, one I hadn't even had the courage to enter before. Both Mrs. Appleton and I were impressed.

Miss Seymour introduced us: "Mr. Lundquist, meet Mrs. Appleton." A demure hand extended, a look of surprise at so young a lawyer. Miss Seymour to the rescue. "Sara: he is the best one for you. He knows the most law of any lawyer here. He just got out of Harvard Law School. And you know that's special, for you don't really need to go to school to practice law." I think Miss Seymour and Mr. Rice held the view that law schools were necessary only for those not possessing an innate understanding of law. Law schools had become like carbon paper and copying machines, necessary but not necessarily best.

Mrs. Appleton had personality traits that, I've come to realize in later years, made her hell to cross examine. She knew what her answer would be, without paying much attention to the questions. From my viewpoint this quality was offset, however, by her propensity to be self-directed under my direct examination. For Widow Appleton, life was theater: Ask her a question and she had a role to act out. Facts have a subjective cast when their predicate is the eye of the beholder.

Mrs. Appleton had stagy eyes. Theater carried to her manner and dress. She was tall, near to spindly, with soft, red, curly hair going to white-gray. Sara possessed the attractiveness of a rose with some thorns to be wary of. Animated in gesture, she wore glasses that kept creeping to the end of her nose, to be returned with a quick push of her finger, then to start again whence they had begun. Her movement as she talked was as regular as a metronome, the beat varying only with the liveliness of the role she was assuming.

Mrs. Appleton had been widowed for some time. She was childless. A quick look might have one call her homely. A second would not. Her supple figure wore garments well that elsewhere might be a few years behind the times but in Worcester were current fashion. Immediately eye catching were the light-toned soft natural fabrics she favored as a careful complement to her coloring. What gave special effect and strength to Mrs. Appleton was an energy of friendliness that swept one in. "You had to like Sara!" "Everyone did!" Patience Seymour prized her as best friend. Others did, too, for she played best friend to many, even if she was close friend to none.

W. Hurlbert Rice uncharacteristically interrupted his day to spend time in a visit and idle chat with us. Miss Seymour was pleased, but Hurlbert moved out quickly, for wasting time was not to be any part of his stock in trade—not at thirty-five dollars an hour. Everyone, it seemed, cared for Sara Appleton, except Mr. Giovannini, the "mover-inner."

"And he is out there day after day . . . bald but trim."

With only the afternoon available to prepare for the morrow's courtroom adventure, I started right in: "Perhaps we could start with the pictures, Mrs. Appleton?"

"I'm afraid not, Mr. Lundquist. Patience said they were for Court. I'll bring them tomorrow."

"Well, yes. Then, tell me about—describe what has happened."

"Mr. Giovannini is an uncouth and unfriendly man. He moved into the former Lane residence last spring. The Lanes were lovely neighbors. Lived there forty years, then they moved to Florida. I'm still in touch."

Addressing the remainder of this report to Miss Seymour, she continued: "Patience, I got another letter and a picture last week. The Lanes are brown as bears. Would you like to see?" She had brought the Lane picture along. I politely shared with Miss Seymour a look at it, finding it difficult to catch their "brown-bear tan" from a black-and-white photo.

"Mrs. Appleton, could you tell me what happened? What did Mr. Giovannini do to flood you and to harm your yard?"

"Mr. Lundquist. If you don't mind, I'll call you Weyman. Weyman, it was awful. Right at the south end of the lower part of the Lane property, Mr. Giovannini dug up for a huge garden this spring. Never even told me anything; he hides from me. Now, when it rains, it just floods me out. It's disgraceful. It's ruined my property. And he is out there day after day, shirt off, muscly man." And to Miss Seymour: "bald but trim, Patience. Quite trim, and browner even than the Lanes in Florida." Miss Seymour could also discern things in the Lane photos not visible to my eye.

"What has he said about this to you?"

"Nothing. We don't—we have never talked. I don't even know if he speaks English. He's Italian, you know."

"Well, yes, but could we be a little more specific about what happens, when it happens, and what it does to your property value?"

"Weyman, I have to tell this in court tomorrow, don't I?"

"Yes, you do."

"Good. Let's do it just once then. I don't want to waste your time, and it is costing me money. So we'll do it then." And, turning to my instructing solicitor, Miss Seymour: "Patience, thank you for having me up for such a nice visit, and I do think Weyman is an excellent lawyer. Where is it we go tomorrow?"

Miss Seymour had that all typed out. "Courtroom 5, Department 2. Trial before Chief Municipal Court Judge William Cleary. Be there at 9:25," she instructed Sara. "The trial doesn't start until 9:30." No one exceeded Patience in her parsimonious care of the legal hour. Miss Seymour would waste neither Mrs. Appleton's time nor mine.

"Who is Judge Cleary, Weyman? Tell me about him before I run," inquired Mrs. Appleton in parting. My four weeks in the office and several trips to file things in court hadn't steeped me in the lore of Judge William Cleary. Patience Seymour again took the lead.

"He's a fine man," she said, "though Irish. He's been at the bar almost as long as Mr. Rice, and they sort of know each other socially, at bar association meetings and such." (This deserves a note of explanation in that Hurlbert was a stalwart of the Commonwealth Club, which had been around for over a hundred years prior to Hurlbert's birth. The Commonwealth Club had yet to admit its first minority member. When time forced that change on the august Yankee institution, it reluctantly accepted a Swede and soon thereafter an Irishman, appropriately named Paul Revere O'Connell.)

Miss Seymour was still experiencing discomfort at our role as plaintiff's lawyers. As she explained, "Judge Cleary rules often for plaintiffs. But when he's alert, he does very good things. Why, only last month, he paid attention and gave the maximum sentence to—"

"Mrs. Appleton, I have to go to prepare, and my leaving will save you money. You can visit with Miss Seymour about the judge." My pretrial preparation with the client having set back my trial plans a good deal, I was not about to terrorize myself further by learning of an Irish judge who was good for plaintiffs, apparently when drowsy, but from whom one could expect severe criminal sentences if he paid attention.

The next morning saw that trepidatory walk from 340 Main Street to the granite Worcester County Courthouse. To this day I have the feeling of always walking *up* to get to a courthouse. They are places of natural height. Perhaps this is because the Worcester County Courthouse is literally up on Courthouse Hill at the start of Main Street. More likely, it is because the law is somehow above yet a part of life.

Once over the solid granite steps into the solid granite structure, the feeling changed. Awe and fear commingled. I was in that building to do battle and to win. Yet there is a reverential aspect to battle. The result of all the struggle, the very objective of that strife, is justice. Once caught up in the trial process, lawyers find it a religious experience as well as a professional one. That feeling has never left me. Even today, whenever I enter a small county courthouse or a great federal district court, I gain inner support by visiting the trial lawyers' temples.

Up the stairs to the smaller municipal courts. In judge Cleary's courtroom the judge's wooden bench was elevated. The courtroom furniture—table, chairs, benches—were of oak, old enough to have already served a hundred years, strong enough still to be young for their work of supporting people. The flags, Bay State and American, were positioned respectively to the left and right of the judge's bench. Trying cases was then considered men's work and brass spittoons graced the judge's platform and served counsel's tables. In the back benches were the inevitable hangers-on , people for whom life is the courtroom and its processes. Every courthouse has such followers.

In this, my first courtroom venture, I feared the known: Judge Cleary, the Banducci firm's talent, Mrs. Appleton's lack of preparation, my own abysmal ignorance. And the unknown! Judge Cleary: asleep or alert? What talent from the Banducci office? What would Mrs. Appleton say? And what could I do?

It was a bright October morning. I felt alive to its every nuance—snapping blue sky, wisps of cloud spotting the sunshine. Outside, the air was Indian-summer cooled. Inside, it seemed used-up and old. I wanted to be anywhere but in that courthouse. Yet, inexorably, I was drawn to it. Mrs. Appleton had a story to tell. Mr. Giovannini had a reply. Blind Justice waited to have her scales tipped. And, by God, if nothing else, Banducci's hired gun (even then I knew the opposition was the other lawyer, not his or her client) would know he was in for a scrap!

The Central District Municipal Court in Massachusetts handled civil matters involving lesser amounts, never lesser problems, as Herbert Holmquist, chief administrator of that court, often told me. Herb Holmquist was well known to me. In the ethnic balance that ran Worcester—Yankees, Swedes, Irish, and Italians—the later arrivals, particularly Swedes and Irish, through the buoyancy of votes were increasingly surfacing in governmental positions. Clerk of the Central District Municipal Court was a plum among these jobs. While, occasionally and when in deep trouble, civil or criminal voters got to the high trial jurisdiction of the Supreme Judicial Court, everyday matters were brought into Herb Holmquist's domain. Saturday night drunks, juvenile disturbers (not criminals to Herb; their parents voted), family disputes, failures to pay for the sofa bought from Denholm & McKay's, barroom fights, traffic offenses, all came his way— not a few, not dozens, but hundreds. I suspect that his court's docket was no less filed against than those we describe as "overly litigious," "crowded calendars," of delay and inefficiency today. Herb Holmquist, however, "The Chief," was the sieve through which it all flowed, and he saw that it moved along.

Mr. Holmquist, at times called "Your Honor" when he sat as the clerk with power over some petty criminal matter, sorted it all out. He decided whether there was probable cause for arrest, when criminal cases might be set (if he didn't like the crime, it would be set when the arresting officer was on vacation), what judge would handle a civil matter, and the availability and makeup of a jury panel. On occasion he personally consulted with clients on their family disputes, "not with you lawyers, damn it—with the people involved."

Holmquist grew affluent in the process, for each night booking brought a two-dollar fee to the Chief, who somehow didn't need to be there to "book them." To hang on to this post, Herb needed solid Swedish support. He also needed to keep the old-line Yankees mollified and, at a minimum, to retain respect of the Irish and Italians, each of whom controlled their own legal bailiwicks, be they the registry of deeds, the probate court, or the police station and bond houses. To achieve this, each ethnic community had its own lawyer-statesman-diplomat-officeholder. For the Swedes, it was Holmquist. Herb knew me well, for there were only four Swedish lawyers in Worcester. More importantly he knew my large, voting family.

Through "Chief" Holmquist, I hoped for a leg up on my Banducci foe, since Herb was a Swede, and ethnic ties ran tight in Worcester. In fact, I had scouted Judge Cleary with Mr. Holmquist and had received valuable advice. "Be on time. Speak up. Call the judge "Your Honor." Listen to what he says. Answer his questions, not yours. Don't argue after he has said something. Ask the clerk to mark the exhibits. Show the exhibits to the judge. Bring a law book if you've got a case. Put on your best evidence in the morning. He is partial to ladies and Irish policemen." His list went on, still pertinent for most courtrooms albeit calling for some modifications, judge by judge.

Mrs. Appleton and the clerk's call arrived simultaneously at 9:30.

"*Appleton vs. Giovannini.*"

"Weyman Lundquist, Your Honor. Ready for the plaintiff." Good so far.

And from nearby, "Mr. Ryan, Judge. Francis Ryan for Mr. Giovannini."

Damn Banducci! Tricky already! An Irish lawyer for an Irish judge. But I had Mr. Holmquist to count on.

"Good morning, Mr. Ryan. It's a pleasure to see you other than in church!"

"And good morning, Mr. Lundquist. I haven't had the pleasure of meeting you, and *rarely* do I have the presence of fine lawyers from Mr. Rice's firm *here*." Was Mrs. Appleton impressed? Should I be? Was it a put down or a point up?

"Mr. Holmquist and I have talked about this trial. He tells me there is a shortage of jurors, and I know equity is involved, so there'll be *no* jury."

Jointly: "Yes, Your Honor."

While Giovannini obtained an Irish lawyer for an Irish judge, Mrs. Appleton's plaintive plaintiff's Swedish lawyer couldn't even get a jury trial for her. The Lundquist voting bloc would be reconsidering Herb Holmquist.

"Gentlemen, unless you insist, we'll waive openings. I've read the pleadings and know what the case is about."

Again, in chorus: "Yes, Your Honor." Frank Ryan, also employed in his first trial, was as grateful as I to forgo opening statements. Later over a post-trial coffee, I said to Frank, "Thank God the judge ruled out openings." Ryan inquired, "What in hell is an 'opening'?" I couldn't tell him.

"Call your first witness, Mr. Lundquist."

"I only have a first witness, Judge—Your Honor."

"Well, call her, son."

William Cleary had been at the bar a long time and on the bench for thirty years. It was not for lack of talent that he had risen through civil service work in City Hall while attending night law school. He became a criminal defense lawyer, successful at dealing with prosecutors and at beguiling Irish-cop witnesses into favoring his clients just a little. Cleary was able to win the respect of jurors—Yankees, Irish, Swedes, Italians. In a polyglot city, thirty years earlier when an appropriate administration was in power, he received a deserved appointment as a municipal court judge.

It was a judge that William Cleary had wanted to be all his life. He graced the office. No retirement for him. He enjoyed the prestige and the quiet respect that is given by power over the lives of people in their matters of daily concern. Family disputes, drunken driving, small criminals, and civil discord, which are each day the lifeblood of our courts, coursed through his judicial veins. He, along with the Herb Holmquists, Buzzy Banduccis, and even the Hurlbert Rices, kept the system alive and well. While there might be many filings, it was the cases tried and results obtained that benchmarked the justice delivered. And however it was obtained, this system worked and had the respect of the Worcester community. Swedes could accept arrest by Irish cops, even as Irish cops could accept Herb Holmquist's setting trials they could not attend. The important thing was that the system deliver justice the community could live with. It did.

Well into his seventies, Judge Cleary was never jaundiced by his work. He was less interested in highly paid lawyers or in complicated law than he was in facts. With facts came the ability to solve or, if not to solve, at least to adjust people's problems.

Judge Cleary did not worry over appeals. "First, because," as he later told me, "there are very few appeals from municipal courts. Second, because I am where I want to be and no higher court can affect that. And, finally, because I don't have the time or interest to explain why my decisions are right and the high court's wrong. I'm too busy with justice to worry about law."

Mrs. Appleton was sworn.

Let me forsake the transcript to summarize early impressions. Pleasant widow, unmitigatingly friendly, charming, attractive, and gracious. Ever lonesome for a friend despite so many friends. She had lived in her Highland Street neighborhood for many years. Mr. Giovannini was a "newcomer." He had moved from a Shrewsbury Street flat just a year ago so that he could have a garden and a yard.

Despite Mrs. Appleton's patrician qualities, the judge liked her. As I made inquiry, Ryan tried an objection or two.

"Mrs. Appleton, when the rains came, it caused the water to flood from Mr. Giovannini's garden to your yard, did it not?"

"Leading, Your Honor."

"Perhaps so, Mr. Ryan, but I can evaluate it."

"Ambiguous question, Your Honor. And it calls for a conclusion."

"Well, it may be ambiguous to you Counsel but I understand it, and I'll make my own conclusions."

And when appropriate, Judge Cleary offered his own good questions: "The rows of this garden run north to south, do they not, Mrs. Appleton?"

"Yes, Your Honor."

Ryan and I were both learning. Ryan had the sense not to object to the Judge's leading inquiries. I proceeded.

"And now, Mrs. Appleton, have you taken some pictures?"

"Yes, Weyman—Mr. Lundquist."

"Mr. Clerk, would you mark them, please?"

"Plaintiff's 1, 2, and 3."

"Thank you. We offer these, Your Honor."

Ryan was restive, but uncertain as to what to do. The judge, ready to help us both, inquired: "And before I admit these, Mrs. Appleton, can you assure me that they fairly and accurately represent the Giovannini property where the garden is and the damage to your own yard?"

"Well, the first two do, Your Honor. But the third one of my yard is bad. It makes things look much worse than they are."

"Fine. One and two admitted. Three for identification only. Let me see them, Mr. Clerk. Proceed, Mr. Lundquist."

Slowly, what had happened sunk in. Mrs. Appleton had proved herself honest, but that her property was not damaged. However, the judge had seen all the evidence, admitted or not, and could make his own assessment of damage. I was beginning to enjoy my line of work, although in fact the pictures showed distressingly little harm except for the one not admitted.

We covered more facts—Mr. Giovannini's digging the rows which ran north and south, straight up and down the hill; the size of his tomatoes; Mr. Giovannini's industriousness and his inhospitality. "We've never been introduced." "No one in the neighborhood knows him."

Finally, the heart of our case, damages. I had done my research for this one. "Prove the properties before and after value," the books said. "The owner can do it." My recollection was that an early *Goldstein on Trial* even gave the exact questions. I was rote-ready with questions written out.

"Who owns the property at 7 Highland Street?"

In a surprised tone: "Why, you know I do, Mr. Lundquist."

"Mrs. Appleton, do you have an opinion of its value this spring, before Mr.Giovannini put in his garden which flooded you and harmed your property?"

(Ryan was of uncertain objection; the judge, tolerant.)

"I do."

"Do you have an opinion of your property's value after Mr. Giovannini and the flooding?"

"I do."

"Do you have an opinion as to the dollar amount of the damage to your property?"

"I do."

"How much?"

"Two hundred and fifty dollars."

(I could at least have let Ryan do the follow-up, but flushed with easy success, I improvised.)

"And what was the value of your property before Mr. Giovannini arrived?"

"Forty-three hundred dollars."

"And after his arrival and the flood?"

"Forty-five hundred dollars."

The judge, morning alert, "Forty-five hundred, Mrs. Appleton! Did you say $4,500? More after the flood?"

"Yes, Your Honor."

Facts were coming out faster than I could quite handle. The judge was nonplussed. Trying to resurrect whatever there was to be resurrected, I plunged on. "What accounts for the value difference, Mrs. Appleton?"

"Why, Mr. Giovannini set new highs for a purchase price when he bought his house. The entire neighborhood went up in value."

Desperately: "But you are certain your property has been damaged by $250. Why?"

"I am. I just know it."

Ryan, "Objection. No foundation in fact."

Judge Cleary: "Objection overruled. Mrs. Appleton's knowledge speaks for itself."

Sara Appleton beamed. I did not.

"You may inquire, Mr. Ryan."

Francis Ryan had been as confused as I about all this and had no more experience, but he knew that Banducci's lawyers went for the jugular. He proceeded to do so.

"Mrs. Appleton, you don't like Mr. Giovannini, do you?"

Lundquist, "Objection."

Mrs. Appleton, proceeding anyway: "I don't know him. Mr.—Mr.—is it Ryan?"

Lundquist: "Withdrawn."

Mrs. Appleton, "I've never been introduced. He does seem nice enough. I'd like to meet him."

After that start, Ryan's questions meandered. Sensibly, he kept them short. He stopped, then called Mr. Giovannini to be sworn. Mr. Giovannini, right hand raised haltingly, read the oath proferred by the clerk. He swore to tell the truth.

Ryan on direct: "Please tell us your name."

Ignoring Ryan, Mr. Giovannini turned to the judge.

"Your Honor? Adolfo Giovannini."

"Yes, Mr. Giovannini."

Now, reaching into his pocket, "I'm sorry. Here's the $250. The lady, she never told me I hurt her."

Sara Appleton, from the plaintiff's counsel table: "Well, Your Honor, I couldn't take his money. I don't even know Mr. Giovannini."

Judge Cleary: "Order, please! The case is submitted. My opinion will be issued within a week. Thank you, Mrs. Appleton and Mr. Giovannini. I commend you for the excellent lawyers you've had here representing you. Both, from distinguished firms, presented your cases as few could have. Court's in recess."

Neither Mrs. Appleton nor Mr. Giovannini seemed surprised. They had innate confidence in Judge Cleary. Ryan and I, however, were amazed. After introducing our clients to shake hands and part, we repaired to the courthouse coffee shop to ponder what the judge might do.

Judge Cleary's written decision came down in due course: "It is hereby determined that Sara Appleton has been substantially damaged by Mr. Adolfo Giovannini's activities but in a *de minimis* dollar amount because the market value of her property has been enhanced by Mr. Giovannini's purchase in her neighborhood. However to prevent further harm, Mr. Adolfo Giovannini must hereafter garden from east to west to avoid flooding Mrs. Appleton's property.

"The parties are further ordered to meet in person within thirty days of this Order, with counsel or not, as they determine, to review Mr. Giovannini's gardening plans for the next season. Each side to pay their own costs and their own attorneys."

Miss Seymour thought it a great win. So, Mrs. Appleton must have approved. Ryan told me Mr. Giovannini approved of it. Ryan and I were satisfied because our clients each thought they had won. Mr. Rice liked the expressiveness of the judge's words concerning attorneys' fees.

The last I knew, Mrs. Appleton and Mr. Giovannini were congenial neighbors interested in common gardening pursuits.

Law
at the Edge—
Alaska

After several years of private practice in Worcester, Massachusetts, I joined the United States attorney's office in Boston, self-considered hub of the universe. As an assistant United States attorney, I had the good fortune to work with two eminences of the Massachusetts bar, Elliot Richardson and the Honorable Arthur Garrity. There remain yet in my Sunday recollections numerous war stories from that era, still untold.

After two years, I moved on to the United States attorney's office in Alaska. If you are under forty, the next set of stories may pose a challenge. Especially for those readers over forty, let's revisit the trial lawyers who lived at the time of the Army-McCarthy hearings and the great legal happenings of the late 1950s and early 1960s. All of these were a factor in my move to Alaska.

A preeminent lawyer of the 1950s was the late Joe Welch of Army-McCarthy hearing fame. Joe was late to come to the trial bar. I think he was thirty-nine before he became a lawyer. Prior to the hearings, Welch was well known if not then famous, particularly for his representation of clients in libel matters. Indeed, one good fortune of my Worcester training was to have observed him representing the *Worcester Telegram and Evening Gazette* in a libel trial.

The personality and talent of Joe Welch were a natural foil to Senator Joe McCarthy and his cohorts, Roy Cohn and David Schine. This confrontation became historic because it was the first nationally televised adversary proceeding. It made a trial lawyer into a national figure. For law students of that era it did two things. It enhanced the meaning of what it was to be a trial lawyer, and it reaffirmed the respectability and responsibility of standing up on principle for unpopular causes. This was something trial lawyers had heard about. It's part of the folklore of the profession. But in an era when Joe McCarthy intimidated many strong souls by smearing individuals with Communist allegations, Joe Welch's standing up honorably, unafraid, and with appropriate moral indignation through his lawyering gave credence to our profession. Joe Welch's TV debut marked one of the reasons for the rise of the trial bar in the post-World War II era.

Following Welch and the Army-McCarthy hearings, justice became respectable. The Eisenhower administration put ethics before politics. Indeed, Sherman Adams, then Eisenhower's closest White House aide, was dismissed because he took as a gift one vicuna coat. The self-conscious morality of that era caused this high White House official to be discharged for matters that today would probably not keep an attorney general out of office.

This age of incorruptibility was graced in 1960 by the Kennedy administration and its readiness to take on any cause and any foe in the pursuit of justice for the people. It inaugurated one of the inspirational epochs of our profession. For a prosecutor, those were heady times. The enemies were discrimination, corruption, organized crime, and business cheating. The public assumed that prosecutors sought true

justice. As is often the case, that assumption shaped professional conduct and the Kennedys' brief ascension marked an
enthusiasm and effort by government lawyers and civil ser-
vants unparalleled in this lifetime.

Working in the United States Attorney's office in Boston
under both Republicans and Democrats in the late 1950s and
early 1960s was rewarding work. Judges were good—
demanding, but fair. Lawyer professionalism was a given.
The courtroom was not for the lazy, the timid, or the dull. I
smarted sorely when Judge Charles Wyzanski once quipped
that I pursued a case as a persecutor, not a prosecutor. The
prosecutor was not merely charged with winning; he was
charged with winning ethically, and for a proper cause.

United States attorneys played their offices like violins. Tax
fraud cases were seasonally brought, the season being tax
return time. The defendants were selected deliberately, phar-
macists, doctors and contractors—so that the public would
give full attention to their tax returns. And the cases were
publicized. There were grand-jury investigations of corruption, sometimes directed by a judge himself. There was attack
after attack on organized crime. If the prosecutors could not
act fast enough, television would. On one occasion, CBS-TV
was preparing the documentary of a bookie operation in
Boston. To prevent embarrassment, the United States attorney's office feverishly hastened to raid the shop for the documentary, "Diary of a Bookie," all to the end that crime in
Boston's streets not be first exposed on television. In the early
Kennedy days even Democratic politicos could be target defendants. The Teamsters, and especially James Hoffa were
under onslaught. Assistant United States attorneys operated,
confident that their work was on the side of truth, beauty,
and justice.

And we worked and worked and worked more. Our goal
was to get ten years of trial experience packed into two or
three years. In a bipartisan office, one could achieve a career
reputation after two or three years of successful prosecuting.

Competition was not only with the defense bar but with one's peers. The reward was a position as trial lawyer with a major firm, or in one's own practice, or a seat on the bench.

I was lucky to work on cases involving everything from unwitnessed accidents on the Charles River bridge to Russian trawlers invading Georges Bank to indicting and convicting the mayor of Everett, Massachusetts. Along the way was the Bernard Goldstein tax fraud case with Edward Bennett Williams magnificently handling the losing defense, while Elliot Richardson became the successful prosecutor. There were organized crime raids against bookies. There were even thousands of mink killed, a slaughter allegedly caused by low-flying, sonic-booming Air Force planes. It was rollicking fun, but physically and mentally demanding work. While the hours were atrocious and the pay paltry, the work was exhilarating, and the reward was the ideal training for a chosen career. Assistant United States attorneys considered themselves among the law's anointed—a perception that still survives.

From my labors in this interesting legal vineyard I came to find the trial court a comfortable place, my arena of choice. From the outset, I had planned to return to my firm in Worcester, using the seasoning of my assistant United States attorney's experience to further my law career. Although I was now ready to return to private practice, I proposed that if government service had something really interesting that would require an assistant United States attorney as a trial lawyer, I might consider staying on. One month later, I was asked to go to Alaska to handle tax and security fraud prosecutions there. It was an offer I could not refuse.

The change from the staid federal courthouse of Boston, with its rigorous decorum, to the courthouses of Alaska, in Nome, Ketchikan, Juneau, and Anchorage, was dramatic. Alaska had just become a state. There was no state-generated law on its books. Indeed, it had a history of lawlessness, or at least unusual law. Nevertheless, Alaska liked law and it liked lawyers. It was prepared then, as it had been historically, to abide by law's rules as long as they were Alaska's laws and Alaska's rules. There I first discerned that part of the genius of our legal system was America's ability to govern its citizens through laws developed in each state and applied by local jurors. In such a setting it is the trial advocate's responsibility to use the system's rules to focus for the courtroom the facts that will see the law of that jurisdiction applied for the client.

Alaska itself was a great adventure, its beauty awesome, varied, frightening. Its climate was challenging, but invigorating and diverse. I met people who were transitory souls with an extraordinary zest for life. My parents' having journeyed several thousand miles from Sweden to Worcester, Massachusetts, for a new start made it a logical extension for me, in some Viking way, to try my craft as lawyer on the Alaska frontier. It would be an unforgettable experience.

The
Nome-Kotzebue
Bar

O n occasion I have claimed to possess the widest range
of courtroom experience in America, Nome and Boston being about five thousand miles apart. While I
started in the Worcester courts to gain experience and was
seasoned further in the Boston federal district court, it was
in Alaska that I got my important lead counsel experience.

To get to Nome, then as today, inevitably involves air travel.
In earlier times, the principal overland link was water, or one
could travel by foot or dogsled. Even today, during each
winter some hardy souls get from Fairbanks to Nome by
dogsled on the Iditarod Trail. Dogsled transit was dramatized
in 1925 when dog runners dashed some 647 miles from Nen-
ana (then the last rail point) to Nome with serum to fight
the polio epidemic raging there. In typical Alaska fashion,
even the account of that high adventure is confused about
who are the real heroes. Amusingly, the lead dog—"Balto,
the dog hero"—of the Nome serum run is enshrined in New
York's Central Park. Balto was not even on the team driven
by Leonhard Seppala, the most famous of the serum-race

dog mushers. Seppala was regarded as the most important (about ninety-three miles' worth) of the twenty mushers who participated in that January, 1925, excursion at temperatures dipping to forty-two below zero. Having the hero dog on one team and the hero musher on another is a bit like having the plaintiff and defendant at odds, with each coming out neither as victor nor vanquished. The legal adventure I am about to describe was not unlike that.

Dogsled is not the only overland transit route to Nome. One of the more notable involved an eleven-hundred-mile bike ride by a Norwegian, Edward Jesson, in March, 1901, from Dawson City to The Golden Beach of Nome. Jesson found himself faster than most of the dogsled travelers and all of the hikers. Despite this record, bicycling overland in the Arctic remains out of vogue as a sport. Jesson's glorious bit of exercise was undertaken, of course, in pursuit of the coveted gold sought in Nome by all.

With treasure, even in those early times, came lawyers, the outriders of commercial fortune. Then, as now, the law's focus turned to obvious if not easy dollars. Nome was awash with citizens described as "having special criminal vocations," "thieves," "gamblers," "general crooks," "all-around crooks," "confidence men," "train robbers" (not very smart ones: some 647 miles from the station), "pickpockets," and "clever pickpockets," to quote the descriptions of the Northwest Mounties of that day. Some were members of the O'Leary Gang from Skagway, or "Soapy Smith's gang," along with other robust robber organizations. With Nome's clientele, Butte, Montana, which had until then been viewed as America's wickedest city, was comparatively described by the United States attorney general's special agent in Nome as a "righteous and law-abiding community."

Because Nome then lacked the technical legal right to create a municipal government (congressional permission being required), it operated at the suggestion of Alaska District Judge Charles Johnson by a consent form of government. Because law compliance was voluntary, tax collection under the auspices of young Ky Pittman, the first city attorney, became an art.

As tax funds ran out in 1901, the city government did two things. Both seem consistent with the actions of our enlightened, contemporary, sophisticated politicians. On the one hand, to raise revenue, they levied a tax on prostitution and gambling. On the other, they convened a grand jury, which concluded that lawlessness in Nome was caused largely by women in saloons and gambling halls. Their edict: Ban them.

From such dubious legal reasoning, it was easy to advance the next step: to arrange the appointment of a weak and crooked judge, Arthur Noyes. Noyes would focus his attention on obvious crime while permitting, as a matter of legal sufferance, true grand larceny. The grand larceny lay in taking legal gold claims from their miner owners. This puppet judge had his strings pulled by Alexander "The Great" MacKenzie, of Rex Beach's *Spoilers* fame. False claims, trespass, misuse of fiduciary funds, and securities fraud were the touchstones of MacKenzie's larcenous adventures. The result, as W. E. Lillo, chief historian of the times, later wrote: "The manner in which the promoters of this enterprise escaped the vengeance of the law has no parallel in the crime annals of the country." It was into this richly chaotic tradition of jurisprudence that I traveled in 1961.

The federal judicial District of Alaska was the nation's largest and most sparsely populated. We had plenty of federal courthouses in Juneau, Ketchikan, St. Petersburg, Anchorage, Fairbanks, and Nome, among others, but only one judge, United States Federal District Court "Judge H," for Homer Waterloo Hodge. Thus, in Alaska, while the courthouses remained *in situ* sometimes thousands of miles apart, justice—in the form of judge, clerks, marshals, reporters, and lawyers—traveled.

One of my first trial assignments was to Nome, where both lawyers and lawlessness had survived. My first trip "in" to western Alaska was with a veritable Chaucerian legal entourage. There was the diminutive Judge Hodge protected by the even smaller United States marshal, Clement Coleburn. Transcribing the judge's words was Mable Wynot, the judge's court reporter. Mable was returning home to Nome, where she had lived as a child, had seen the great Leonhard Seppala driving the serum in, and read Nome's history firsthand from the pages of the *Nome Nugget,* Alaska's oldest newspaper, "published daily except Monday, Tuesday, Wednesday, Friday, Saturday, and Sunday." Last and least was Weyman I. Lundquist, out-of-court porter for Judge Hodge and, in court, the assistant United States attorney. My most usual task was as a criminal prosecutor, a favored role in the eyes of most of the populace, who wanted bad criminals arrested and jailed. Good ones, defined as relatives, friends, or loved ones, were to be left alone. This time, unfortunately, I was wearing my civil hat and the mantle of defender of the purse of the United States of America—in this instance, defending it from Arthur McPherson's 1960s search for gold in Nome.

My dual courtroom missions produced ambivalent reactions. By and large, the judge, the marshal, and most of our group favored my capacity as prosecutor. Anyone bad enough to get arrested in Nome damn well deserved jail. The culprits were not anonymous villains but, rather, well-known offenders. If the marshal or local state trooper, each responsible for thousands of square miles of territory, had to go to all the trouble of making an arrest, conviction should follow.

Contrariwise, in civil matters, opinion was unanimous that my client, the United States, was miserly and out of touch with the realities, needs, and expense of life in Alaska. My trying to hang onto federal funds had all the popularity of the temperance movement in Nome, where a winter's evening at a bar lasted several months.

My perceptions in this regard were confirmed when I was invited, through a mutual friend, to take sherry and dine with Edith Crowley, grande dame of the Nome province. Edith was a tough lady. I had learned of her from a Coast Guard captain in Boston. He told me if I ever got to Nome there was a special person I must meet. I knew that Edith had worked her way up to Nome as a cook on a tugboat and then up in the business world of Nome to owning and presiding over the North Star Tug and Barge Company, one of Nome's major enterprises. As a Bering Sea admiral, Edith's contacts were far reaching; and from my Eastern friends she had learned of my pilgrimage to Alaska.

Edith was anxious to meet me, recently of Boston. She wanted to learn of her old friends there and to share with me her abiding love of the awesome arctic country that was her home. I had expected hot coffee, hopefully a shot or two of whiskey and a kitchen-table meal, if I were lucky. I had walked from the North Star Hotel down the frozen-mud main street over the permafrost tundra to the large two-story warehouse shed of the North Star Tug and Barge. Climbing the outside stairs to Edith's apartment, I entered another world.

Hers was an immense domicile. I was led into a tastefully furnished grand room, with fine rugs on its polished floors and dominated by an eye-catching, wonderful crystal chandelier suspended over a walnut dining table. It was the only chandelier north of the Arctic Circle. Edith, a stately lady even after decades of life in Nome, produced a fine bottle of Spanish sherry, poured for each of us a generous portion, instructed me to pull up a chair, that we each might look through the room's large window at the Bering Sea and watch. In silence, we savored the sun's slow April evening flirtation with the arctic skyline, as the endless night of winter gave way to the season of days that never end.

I sensed Edith wanted to talk, and I most assuredly wanted to listen and understand how the Arctic Circle and the tin huts and outpost buildings of Nome had enchanted Edith Crowley. But direct questions of a lady were contrary to my Boston experience. Somewhere, too, it lurked in my memory that Mrs. Crowley, like so many other Alaskans, had parts of a past which they might tell about, but about which no one inquired. So I started innocuously with the "do you like it here?"

We savored the sun's slow April flirtation with the arctic skyline.

Her sherry remained untouched. The light of the spring-climbing arctic sun, sending rays almost flat into the room from the western rim of the world, gave a luminescence to Edith, as did her words. I don't recall them precisely, but they painted pictures for my mind. Edith was Boston-born of Irish immigrant parents, and was orphaned early. There she learned that there were qualities important to a lifestyle and that among them was bright stimulation for the mind, lest one become stifled. She learned, too, that for her, Boston would not permit that opportunity.

Somehow she migrated west, not in any one move, nor in any one occupation she chose to describe. She finally reached San Francisco shortly after the earthquake. What she did in San Francisco was never clarified, but she was a player. She knew where the fine restaurants of old were, as well as the colorful society leaders of high and low estate. Whatever happened there, San Francisco was not to her ultimate taste. By the 1930s, the Depression's gray hues crept into the picture. Then came a new opportunity, one more chance to move west again, and she found the two true loves of her life: tugboat owning Captain Jack Crowley and the Arctic. The three were made for each other, and that April evening I shared the warm glow of her love for Captain Jack, who had left, and for the Arctic, which will always be there.

Edith had responded to a *San Francisco Chronicle* ad for adventure, work, and the North. That ad sought a cook for Captain Crowley's *North Star* tug. Edith, by then certainly in her forties, sought the position. How well she could cook may have been questionable, but there was no doubt that from the first, Jack Crowley, then in his sixties, and Edith hit it off.

Life on a tugboat hauling freight to Nome left little time for slow niceties. Within a year, they married. Within three years, they settled in Nome. Then the war and the cold-war aftermath produced for their tug business a military support industry that made the Crowleys' fortune. With Jack's advancing years, Edith more and more ran the business, which was by now a small fleet of tugs: first as Mrs. Captain Jack, then in her own right as Captain Edith.

It was she, with Jack's total support, who planned, furnished, and came to treasure their Nome dwelling. In it, she lived with the style she had longed for. It was where she found the time for her mind's stimulation that Boston never would have permitted. The Arctic had produced the Crowleys' wealth, but more significantly it had become the place where their lives achieved that delicate balance of work, home, love of person, and love of environment that so few achieve.

Almost embarrassed at the quiet richness of her own story, Edith turned to discuss my visit there. The *Nome Nugget*'s leading story had disclosed my purpose in Nome: "to take for the U.S. of A., Arthur McPherson's Gold Claims for little or nothing for Federal Aviation Purposes." It went on to report that while "taking land for aviation was fine, but to jump a man's claim should, at the least, take a lot of scratch." In a land where permanent residents with a choice stayed in Nome because of their dream of wealth through gold, taking a man's claim for "small scratch" was perfidy beyond even America's departure from the gold standard.

As the sherry warmed my insides, Edith shared information on the lawyers of the Nome-Kotzebue region and on Frank Croft, my opponent of the morrow. Edith knew everyone North of the sixty-sixth parallel as few did. Really, the only resident lawyer in the vast region was Croft; the few other lawyers who graced Nome's court came in for specific cases from Fairbanks, and on occasion even from Anchorage.

Apart from his geographic presence, lawyer Croft was interesting to the point of notoriety. In a community that was weather-locked for seven or eight months, gossip and liquor filled the long winter. Frank Croft provided grist for the fireside as well as the gin mill. Frank, as rumor had it—a rumor that, as rumor had it, was inspired by Frank—began his practice of law at the Idaho bar some decades past when Idaho was active gold-mining country. Some contretemps there involving gold-mining disputes led to his Idaho disbarment. His early legal escapades demonstrated expertise in how law was practiced in the Nome area and provided the basis for his *pro hac vice* admission to the Nome courts on a case-by-case basis. With this temporary entry, Frank did enough work in the Nome-Kotzebue area to establish a prescriptive right to status as an Alaska lawyer. In due course, this prescriptive right, which Frank had used in a very adversarial, open, and (it is fair to say), notorious manner, permitted lawyer Croft to apply for and be given full title to an Alaska legal ticket.

The now-sherry-inspired Edith explained that Frank could never be taken lightly in court. "Eighty-five percent of the local population are Eskimo and will be called as jurors. You can expect a majority of Eskimos on the jury. Frank knows them all. He has represented many and has acted like a father to even more." Then, with the knowing smile of a woman who had enjoyed the status of queen bee in the male hive of Nome, she reported: "In fact, he may be father to countless children here, in a land where the tradition of graciousness extends both to board and bed for the visitor, and warm beds in Alaska require warm women."

These disclosures did little to raise my Boston-based spirits, even after the good sherry. Bidding Edith good evening, I tromped back to the North Star Hotel to plan my trial strategy for the days ahead.

With me were two expert real-estate appraisers hired to testify for the government. They had comprehensively researched the few land transfers in Nome. "Nome has been fifty years in a depressed real-estate market," one reported. Few gold-mining claims had changed hands, and at scant prices. With the shutdown of the last of United States Smelting and Refining's big dredges, the market didn't look listless—it was dead. On the other hand, we knew that gold did exist. The IRS had levied on Arthur McPherson's grocery store in Kotzebue not because of any dollar profit from that emporium, but because Arthur refused to pay taxes on gold that he took in trade or otherwise acquired. Arthur's reasoning was simple enough: If the United States was off the gold standard, so was he, for tax purposes. What we did have to contend with were gold-dreaming jurors, a dangerous prospect even at thirty-two dollars an ounce. While gold was Nome's industry, albeit an industry totally depressed, the spirits of its dreamers remained high. So our experts aimed for fair values, but on the low side—the usual defense expert-valuation gambit.

Frank Croft, on the other hand, told me bluntly: "Gold is valuable and always will be. Gold is Nome's lifeblood and its heritage. These are great claims, and Arthur wants to be paid because you are taking his mother lode." He spoke in terms of values of twenty thousand dollars for less than a half-acre of land. No property in Nome had ever commanded as high a price, even if it was located on the Golden Beach itself. And that, long ago in a time of gold standards and no government-mandated thirty-two dollars an ounce. There was no basis for settlement, I thought. My thinking was reinforced by Frank's known stubbornness, or "integrity," as he defined it. Frank, an old gambler, was not about to be bluffed. He'd stated his figure, and his reputation was involved. Frank would roll the dice.

By this time, I had come to accept Frank's representations that he had no experts. "Why should I?" he said. "Who knows more about the value of Nome gold claims than the people of Nome?" My legal knowledge, supported by the assembled experts, led us to surmise that Arthur McPherson as owner would testify. This April evening, I tried to review with my experts what we might expect.

We had checked Arthur out. He had the luck of five cats. His brother Bill had died in Nome's first fatal auto accident. It was a truly unique accident, because there was only one car in Nome. Bill McPherson drove the Model T through a hole in the icebound Bering Sea. Arthur was mad as hell about the loss of the car, but consoled himself in inheriting his brother's holdings. Arthur, convinced from that early

124

time that automobiles were dangerous, had been one of the first above the Circle to take up flying.

Arthur taught himself to fly and proudly billed himself "the worst flier in Alaska still living." He was legendary for his insistence during World War II on refusing to learn simple pilots' codes concerning weather to prevent radio-broadcast disclosure to the Japanese. Hundreds of miles from either Nome or Fairbanks, his only two airports of call, Arthur would start demanding local weather conditions, only to be refused time and again with, "wartime rules—no weather—use code please." Arthur's fulminations on one particularly bad ice-fog day were legend. He kept firmly insisting on Fairbanks weather and directions as he flew in the general direction of Fairbanks. A stalwart Fairbanks tower operator as adamantly refused to give them. Arthur entreated, cajoled, and swore. Finally, the tower operator replied, "We can do it, but we can do it only if it's an emergency. Is this an emergency?"

Arthur, began at once to shout, "Emergency! Emergency! Emergency!" and received the weather conditions. As he touched down on the Fairbanks runway, he peevishly advised the tower, "*Any*time Arthur McPherson is flying a plane, it's a goddamned emergency!"

His propensity for good luck under adverse conditions was further evidenced in still another flying adventure. This time, his plane hit a tree with its propeller. The wooden shaft broke at one end, bringing Arthur's craft to a tumultuous stop as the prop whirred violently out of sync. Arthur got out, coolly surveyed the situation, took a small hatchet from his gear, chopped off a portion of the unbroken blade, fired up the engine, and took off with the propeller "trued up." So miraculous an engineering accomplishment was this, that on learning that an airplane's wooden propeller could be "trued up with a hatchet only once in a thousand times," Arthur enshrined his engineered marvel over the counter of his Kotzebue grocery store along with a moose head. Arthur was lucky not only on land and in the air but also in love, for he had a fine long-term relationship with Beatrice Abrams, his mistress.

Beatrice Abrams was the only daughter of the union of Joshua Abrams and Beulah Montuk, a full-blooded Eskimo. The Montuk family had a long heritage as members of the Little Diomede tribe. (Little Diomedes Island is situated 130 miles northwest of Nome but only four miles from Russia's Big Diomedes Island.) Little Diomedes was, during Beatrice's childhood, linked to Nome by ice for more than six months of the year, and by kayak or larger boats during the few months of the limited open water season. Beatrice's upbringing combined the western Judaic intellectualism of her father with the native-wisdom heritage of her mother. Beatrice was a gem. She inherited the best personal traits of both families, as well as Joshua's reasonable estate and the arctic industry and talent of her mother.

When he came to Nome, Arthur McPherson courted Beatrice for three years. Once he truly caught Beatrice's fancy, they began to live together, eventually enjoying two fine sons. Marriage in any traditional sense held no attraction. Indeed, Beatrice was one of the firm view that Christian marriage had screwed up any number of fine relationships in the Nome Province. She preferred the romance involved with being Arthur's mistress. As such, she had remained faithful to him (though that value meant less in the wise and necessary Eskimo heritage of occasional wife-sharing); for Arthur's part, he said, "The whole situation does keep me on edge, but Beatrice gets what she wants." The sons, David and Myron, didn't give a damn about their technical bastard status, for they viewed their father, more given to accounts and finances than to their wilderness interests as "a technical old bastard himself."

The entire McPherson-Abrams family was a distinguished one in the Nome Province. Arthur, who owned both the theater and the general store in Kotzebue, was known as an honest banker with people, if not the U.S. of A. McPherson was imbued with enough arctic bonhomie to be ready to share what he had, even salable goods, when others were in need if not in finances. Arthur, in the language of his Nome friends, had "long cuffs." This very generosity assured that he was inevitably repaid when the tides for his customers changed. No one fared well in the Arctic if he ignored the genuine needs of another. In that harsh land, no matter how blessed a human being was, he could count on needing another's help at some time.

This favored Nome citizen, then, was the owner-expert-adversary I had to contend with. Completing our review of how we could deal with the man from the witness stand, one of the experts said, "But you may not have to."

Puzzled but hopeful, I asked, "What do you mean?"

"Well, the *Nome Nugget*, which prides itself on tellin' it like it is, has an article in this week's edition that says, 'Arthur McPherson and his mistress, Beatrice Abrams, are leaving for a vacation in Seattle.' " A quick meeting with Frank Croft established it as gospel: "Arthur always vacations 'outside' in April; I told him there was no reason to change habits just because of a trial that will only come up once in a lifetime."

How could this be? Had Frank Croft given up? Had silver gin cooled his gold fever? Had the case gone from a troublesome raid on the U.S. Treasury to a neat, clean, solid government win? I felt better. Then, on the following day, the trial began.

First, there was the Nome jury to pick. I consulted with the marshal about an appropriate voir dire approach. We had no criminals to put in jail this trip, so the marshal was holding justice close to his vest. "What shall I ask them? About where they live? About do they own gold claims? What's important?"

"Do you speak Eskimo?"

"No, I don't."

"Well, that *is* important. If you don't speak Eskimo, it don't make a damn what you ask them!" So much for the aid of the United States marshal's office.

The solid feeling of an easy win started to mire itself a bit in the soggy tundra of the Nome jury-selection process. In actuality and retrospect, the jury selection was uneventful. The jurors, all Eskimos and ten of them males, were respectful, warily attentive, and quiet. Marshal Coleburn assured the judge we needed no alternates. April was a no-hunting time, so we could expect to keep our panel.

"In the fall, it's hell," the marshal told me, " 'cause when the geese fly or caribou come near, it's their natural, native instinct for survival and food that prevails over any trial. The U.S. Constitution ain't worth a damn then!"

Looking at the poverty of the Eskimos, and at the government's typical harsh treatment of these Native Americans, made the wisdom of choosing a necessary hunt over legal attendance requirements self-evident. The $3.50-a-day from Uncle Sam might be OK if there were no mouths to feed, but, otherwise, survival needs prevailed.

Frank Croft had practiced in the area so long that he was regarded as part of the natural wildlife. He had no precise domicile, moving from family visits to Arthur Little's Arctic Inn to extended barroom stays. "Half a winter spent in the bar may be in the off court season" according to the bartender at the North Star Hotel. While Frank might be considered part of the local fauna, he was also recognized as a unique species and, above all, a lawyer. People said you could tell it just by the way he looked. Frank Croft, Esq., had something to do with that. He wore a long black overcoat in court and outside, explaining that the older courthouse in Nome and the hall used in Kotzebue for criminal matters were so damned cold that "I've gotten used to this old coat as my courtroom gown." Like some antique-adorned barrister, he complemented this by wigging himself with a floppish, soft, gray cap.

Judge Hodge thought Frank's attire fine for Nome and that it probably would be a good idea elsewhere. The judge allowed as how it was "distinctive and in the British tradition." It meant that a judge could tell the lawyer from his client by the robing process. The differentiation of client and lawyer had on occasion eluded Lower Forty-Eight visiting judges in some of Alaska's legal outposts, where, in looking at two equally disheveled supplicants approaching the bench, eminent jurists had often been forced to inquire, "Which one is the defendant?"

The trial began. As the party with the burden of proof, my opening came first and was fulsome in detail of the facts to come. The Eskimo jurors attended my voice for all of several minutes; then their eyes seemed to glaze over, searching through the windows of the courtroom over the Bering Sea as though toward the U.S. Diomede—as though with good eyes you could see the USSR. I didn't feel that my words about the problem at hand—justice and fair prices for land in Nome—had riveted their attention.

Frank was brief in opening. He addressed most of the jurors by name. Whatever the taboo on that in some courts, Judge Hodge allowed, "If you know someone's name, you use it. It's respectful. And Eskimos get little enough respect from the U.S." The old boy was decidedly not warming up to my client's version of justice. Frank spoke a little more, of "golden beaches," of "wealthy men," and of "dreams of riches the government was taking from your good friend and grocer, Arthur McPherson." A few Eskimo words crept into his opening attack, but nothing, so far as I could ascertain, of moment. The trial, however, was another matter.

My witnesses testified well enough, though again the Eskimo jurors scarcely seemed spellbound. Patient souls though they were, not one dropped off to sleep, and only three whittled or polished ivory as the government's case went in and on.

Frank was equally patient, seldom objecting. Lawyer Croft didn't spend much time chatting with me during recesses, however. He was too busy playing with the young Eskimo children who had accompanied their juror parents to court. "One big happy family," as the marshal described them.

While Frank didn't object, he did, on occasion, offer an aside to the jurors in Eskimo! After a time or two, I tried an objection to his sidebars, with little success since, I "couldn't state the grounds for it," as the judge noted. "In fact," as the judge further noted, "there isn't anything on the record either. The reporter can't take Eskimo, you know."

As my case got longer, so did Frank's Eskimo asides. After a particularly extended one, I tried another objection. Judge Hodge, now at least curious, said, "What did you tell them this time, Frank?"

"Your Honor, I told them to relax, to take things calmly. They are concerned, you know, that this courthouse will sink like the last one." This was literally true. The former courthouse, built in the late 1930s, had been foundationed into the permafrost of the tundra. When they fired up its boilers, it proceeded to melt its way into the permafrost, first sinking, then slowly cracking in the middle. No lives were lost.

"They are afraid this courthouse might go down, too, but I'm reassuring them, asking them to keep calm until the trial's over." And, looking at me: "I've assured them that when justice is done everything comes out right in the end." Frank owned the deck.

That night, we settled the case on Frank's terms less 20 percent. I was not about to test records for high jury awards in Nome coming from Frank's Eskimo jury "family" and their pact to have it "all come out right in the end." As the marshal said to me, "The damage you do know is better than the damage you don't know."

We moved on to Kotzebue and the problems of the IRS Receivership of Arthur McPherson's Grocery there. But that story's for another time.

Law in the Yukon— 1961

I remember the outcome of this one differently from Justice Boochever of the Ninth Circuit Court of Appeals. That is not surprising. Many trial outcomes from the distant past achieve new dimensions of interpretation through a lawyer's recall. Justice Boochever told me within the last year or two that he won this one. I think I won. Whatever winning is, is often a matter of perspective. Could you have settled for more than you won? Did the jury award less than you would have paid? The haze of after-trial evenings in Juneau's Red Dog Saloon, and the ephemeral mystery of what justice really is, especially in places like Juneau, do cloud perceptions. Nevertheless, Boochever and I agree on the basic facts. He is as entitled to write his ending as I am.

Some matters would be stipulated. I represented the United States Internal Revenue Service, almost innately a defendant in the eyes of Alaskans, even when it was bringing the case as the plaintiff, as in this instance. Justice Boochever, then a leading light of the Juneau trial bar, represented the defendant. For the sake of ease and fading recollection, we'll call him Harold Nordstrom, a good Scandinavian name. That Scandinavian affinity was one on which I would not be the least hesitant to trade in asking a jury for Scandinavian morality and in calling for Vikinglike responsibility from Harold Nordstrom in all things—and in this case, particularly, all things male.

To understand this trial, some feeling for Juneau is necessary. Like many state capitals, it was located by political compromise. The logic of Alaska's geography and the logic of a voting population center would have the capital located in Anchorage, some six hundred miles north and west of Juneau. But to locate the capital in Anchorage would rile the citizens of Fairbanks, who, while still farther from Juneau, are more immediately concerned about their rivalry with metropolitan Anchorage and its modern development. So the Fairbanks vote goes for Juneau. The Nome ballot box is another matter. It votes against Anchorage on principle and because a capital in Anchorage makes it too convenient for the city dwellers of Anchorage, who are already too soft. Nomians, with their peculiar logic, would rather travel greater distances to get to the capital than make things easy for people in Anchorage. In addition, Nome finds itself kindred to Fairbanks because they are both farther north than the other Alaska cities and more bush. Add Ketchikan and Wrangell as pro-Juneau for reasons of common industry and because they are smaller and less citified than Anchorage, and you understand how the Alaska voters selected Juneau. Perverse logic: voting at its finest.

Now, Juneau is a fine place in its own right. Of course, no highways link it with any place else. It is uniquely difficult to get to. It is remote from nearly all other cities in Alaska. It gets so much rain that its working populace has negotiated for holidays when the sun shines. One year they had two. Juneau is perched on the side of steep mountains, whose summits are snow-adorned for much of the year. The delicate balance between the rain and snow level produces a springtime dance of avalanches. The avalanches are well appreciated, in that they divert one's attention from the usual dark, wet days.

In the early 1960s, Juneau had more than a reasonable complement of bars, alternative beverages being necessary to take the edge off its abundant water. Its population was locked in by water, weather, and mountains. Air travel existed, but the ride into Juneau's one-directional airport was down a slot between two mountain ranges. (I personally never determined whether I was more at ease when the mountains could be glimpsed as one flew between them, so close that forests seemed to touch wings, or when, more often, the mountains could not be seen and we faithfully relied on the mysterious instrument landing approach, certain that we would come down, but uncertain as to where, how, or if in one piece.)

For all of its natural wonders, Juneau had developed some idiosyncrasies. Its host of saloons were identified as "wet bars" or "dry bars," depending on their location. Half the sidewalks in town had rooftops to keep you dry. The other half did not. A person was inevitably half wet or half dry. In Juneau, half-wet exposure was akin to standing in a cold shower. This required a drink. On the other hand, before leaving a dry sidewalk for the wet one, a drink to minimize the anticipated exposure was considered good form; thus, wet and dry saloons. Further, local wisdom had it that the alternating wet and dry sidewalk exposure enhanced one's ability to handle alcohol from the alternating bars. My observations confirmed all theories.

The bars, which far outnumbered the churches, had as fine a collection of stuffed-animal relics as any hunting club, many of them taken in trade on a "long cuff" bill. The Juneau regulars spent so much time with embalmed wildlife that their own visages, like loving animal-owners who begin to resemble their pets, assumed the expression of moose, bear, caribou, otter, salmon, or trout. Their reactions seemed to follow. I am certain that at least six who looked like bears hibernated for extensive periods in Indian Dick's Saloon dig-

The bars had as fine a collection of stuffed-animal relics
as any hunting club.

134

gings. The salmon and trout look-alikes were known to spawn, and while the caribou customers had regular migratory bar routes, I never confirmed that the otter folk could slide on wet tails.

It's easy to go on about Juneau, and I will just a little more. Resilient, affluent folks lived in small homes that periously climbed the hillsides, their residents ever wary that the predatory waters should rise after all the "damn rain." Like most frontier abodes, the houses were small except for the Governor's Mansion, which was located near, almost adjacent to, the local jail. It could be seen from anywhere in Juneau. Convention would have painted it white, to be etched against the permanent evergreen setting around it. Of course convention had no place in Juneau. It was painted forest green. No one had the full explanation, but it was known that a group of prison trustees had done the work as the gift of an outgoing state governor to his successor.

This, then, was the setting for Harold Nordstrom's persecution, or prosecution, depending on which local paper one read. Harold Nordstrom's proceeding was the first commercial civil fraud case brought in Alaska. Mr. Nordstrom was a businessman in Juneau, employing a dozen or more people. Under the "new-fangled federal regulations" (his term), he was, as a corporate officer, responsible for withholding taxes from his employees and paying the withheld taxes to Uncle Sam.

Harold Nordstrom took the withholding responsibility very seriously. He was, however, less punctilious in remitting the withheld funds to the IRS. In fact, he had used them for a Hawaiian trip with his fluttery wife after she had a nervous breakdown of sorts due to the length of the rainy season in Juneau (twelve months, although there is respite when it snows).

Some experience with Alaska justice in the courtroom, and some advice from able Juneau counselors as we waited out the rain in one watering hole or another, had assisted my decision that we not make this a criminal fraud case and, above all, that we not name the fair Mrs. Nordstrom as a party. A friend, Jerry Shortell, a former assistant United States attorney, forcefully pointed out that, up to that time, no Alaska woman had done one day of time for attempting to get or even obtaining an "Alaska divorce." An Alaska divorce generally involved a mishap with firearms resulting in a dead husband, or, as the old-timers put it, "leveling your old man."

This was not only because women in Alaska were in short supply. Jurors in Alaska respected women, and as the jurors were often males who lived alone, often on boats or in the bush, they had very set views as to what a woman should be and how she should be treated. To make Mrs. Nordstrom a defendant would be unchivalrous of Uncle Sam, not to mention ensuring a loss for me. We elected to deny Mrs. Nordstrom equal treatment under the law and to proceed only against her husband, on the well-known prosecutorial theory that half a win is much better than a total loss.

Harold Nordstrom's defense wasn't that he hadn't taken the money or that he would give it back. It was gone. His defense was that he had been so upset by his wife's need to get outside, to leave their small children, to vacation in Hawaii, to ease her nervous disposition so that there might be peace in the home, that Harold forgot whose money he had, or how much it was, or that it came from taxes others were paying to the United States. He and the missus just headed for Hawaii to clear their minds of Juneau matters. All expenses paid, by Uncle Sam.

Now, going "outside" was a luxury some in Juneau aspired to; but to the grizzled, all-male jury, being tough enough to get to Alaska meant being tough enough to stay there—"at least until you had your own poke to get out with," as one of them later told me in a posttrial conference in Indian Dick's establishment. In addition, any male with a home and children "who he and the missus would leave behind" was a sorry sort of man to old sourdoughs who were pleased to have a sod roof over their heads if it didn't leak too badly.

And Mrs. Nordstrom, a fortyish, buxom blonde, whether comely to an outsider or not, was a beauty to men who sometimes saw women but twice a year. Beauty could be cared for in Alaska as well as Hawaii, and better appreciated. So, the reasons for Harold's vacation travel didn't sit too well with the Juneau jurors.

"But we were prepared to let him go," said the foreman, a Norwegian fisherman from Wrangell. "After all, it was really Uncle's money, and using that's not too bad. And the damned forms do everyone in: Just keepin' 'em dry, much less filling 'em out, drives a man crazy in Southeastern. So, it was pretty likely we weren't going to find a man broke the law because he didn't get some soggy forms in on time or with the necessary funds to go along. But it was his wife that caused us to find against him. Remember what she told us when you questioned her. That story did it. Any man who treated a woman that way has to pay his dues."

Now, what that grizzled foreman-fisherman was talking about, I'm not sure. Mrs. Nordstrom on the stand was, as I've noted, a pleasant, buxom, fortyish woman. From the witness box she demonstrated an unusual ability to dominate her husband through obsequiousness. It was plain that she did whatever he wanted, or she said he wanted, to make him do just what she wanted him to do. One could visualize it:

"What color necktie do you want to wear with your jacket?"

"Will you want supper at 5:30 or 6:00?"

"Do you want tea or coffee?"

Killed with kindness he was, offered everything except *his* own choice. Small wonder the man was uxoriously tied down by strictures and he never understood why. She was such a wonderful woman, the deadly kind.

For the all-male jury, just getting close to a woman was unsettling. One that was clean and not half-drunk was a beatific sight. Despite her deceptively weak veneer, they were eager to be chivalrously impressed by her words.

Under Bob Boochever's leading direct, she told how upset she was, "all shut in that house. Rain, rain, rain, then snow, then rain again."

("So what else was new in Juneau?" said my jury foreman friend. "But it got to her and she got to him!")

"I began to get nervous—irritable. I was mad at the children and at Harold all the time. I took it out on them, but mostly on Harold."

"And how did you do that?" Boochever, Esq., gently inquired.

"I wouldn't talk to him. I cried."

"And?"

"I wouldn't get in bed with him."

This was now a matter of real concern to these jurors, who grew up in a land where women were loved and venerated. In a land where abstinence from women's affections went on and on and on. It was also, however, a land where ladies did not violate confidences and men never asked them to. Certain facts of life were never discussed by females in the presence of males. While morality may have been rough in Alaska, it had its proper limits. This no-sex revelation trespassed those forbidden grounds. And all this in a United States district court where both spectators and newspaper reporters were present. A woman who had had a touch of cabin fever was telling this to defend a man who had been infected by her. The jurors wondered why.

"It got to the point where Harold couldn't think of anything but sex, and I couldn't stand the rain. Finally, he promised he'd take me to Hawaii, and I promised I'd do anything he asked me to. And we went, and now things are just fine. I'm better, and we're happy, and I'm doing everything he asks me to."

"Your witness, Mr. Lundquist."

Plainly, the jury was concerned. Harold Nordstrom had aired his linen in public. Still, a man had his needs. Yet, there are some things a man shouldn't do. Was Harold involved in what his wife had said? Should I cross-examine or argue this? I opted for some soft questioning: "Mrs. Nordstrom, do you care about your husband?"

"I do."

"Yet, you wouldn't love him, in a manner of speaking, unless he took you outside, to Hawaii?"

"In a manner of speaking, that's correct."

"Did you know he didn't have the money, his own money, to pay for the trip?"

"Not really. Money matters are his concern."

"Yet, you did tell him you'd do *whatever he wanted* if he took you to Hawaii?"

"I did."

"And, of course, you've gone over your testimony that you'd give today with Harold?"

"I have."

"Several times?"

"Yes."

"And to go back a bit, you did everything he asked you in Hawaii?"

"Yes."

"And you've done everything he asked you to since your return?"

"Yes."

"And he went over with you the testimony he wanted you to give in this case?"

"Yes."

"Several times?"

"Yes."

"And you've testified today just as Harold asked you to, haven't you, Mrs. Nordstrom?"

"I have, because I promised him I would."

"Thank you."

In that land where women were revered and men were strong unto toughness, asking a woman to do that went too far. Breaking the law might be forgiven, but to ask a woman to exonerate you out of your own scrapes could not.

The jury presented Harold Nordstrom with his IRS bill—in full!

Out East to
Back West

Alaska gets inside you. It sure got inside me. It is a
crazy, wild, loving, exciting place. People there don't
think like people you'll find in other places. You find
a curious amalgam in Alaska. The people are more individ-
ualistic, more property-rights-minded, more conservative,
more gun-toting than any place I know. At the same time,
they are more generous, warmer, kinder, and more outgoing
than people anywhere else I know. They are respecters of
home, fireside, and family, yet tolerant, free-wheeling, and
moderately corruptible. They live in one of the world's dramatic, tough, and tender places and they live there because
of it. They also believe they have a God-given right to "cut
it down, use it up, and shoot it."

The Lower Forty-Eight, all the other states except Hawaii
(which sits as far west and due south of Alaska), are called
"outside." San Francisco is "back west," Japan and the Orient
"out east." From Nome, Russia is next door, just a step across
the international date line, or "flying into Sunday," as Arthur
McPherson use to say when he would fly off on a Saturday

afternoon from Nome to wander across the state line to take a look at Russia.

If I'd stayed longer, Alaska would have become an incurable disease, and I could not have left. As it stands, it gave me a romantic affliction that persists. Should I have left?

The legal whys of my departure are a little easier to give. Alaska law was in ferment, requiring traditional lawyering skills of value, but there was a touch-and-feel sense to the development of law there. This was fun and instructive for the trial lawyer. Alaska's giants of the trial bar seemed on the wane, but it is ever thus. More importantly, I had a pretty good win streak going and wanted to test my prowess in another and, I thought, bigger league—again, a major metropolitan center. Further, the federal district court in Alaska was essentially a one-judge court. With one judge, the case outcomes are pretty predictable. More cases get settled as a result. The bar was small, then under three hundred. Everybody knew everybody. I was smitten with wanderlust.

San Francisco beckoned. I was off for a three-thousand-mile drive down the gravelly Alcan Highway to take and pass the California bar examination *twice* in a one-month period. (Having been eight years out of law school, I decided that I'd double-shoot the bar, taking both the attorney's bar and general bar exams, which were then given within one month of each other.) Then it was time for work.

While I didn't realize it then, the litigation frontier in America was just opening. As a member of the Bar who by his early thirties had some trial experience in the courtroom and before juries, I was ready to head into that trying frontier.

The Closely Held
Expert

Georgina Wilbur Cole died in the early 1960s. She had lived a long, long time. So long, in fact, that the stock composing the bulk of her estate had been given to her by doting parents in 1912, a time when there were no estate or gift taxes. Georgina had hung on to her Wilbur Lumber Company stock since then, living easily in a grand style without eroding principal.

The holdings of the Wilbur Lumber Company were vast throughout the Pacific Northwest, and valuable—so valuable that Georgina's estate and the Internal Revenue Service were millions of dollars apart as to the taxes due. Unlike my earlier years in Alaska, when I was charged with defending or enriching the government's coffers, this time I had the more enjoyable task of getting money back from the government, for Georgina's stock had been sold and the tax paid. With Georgina dead, her estate was seeking millions by way of refund. In fact at the time the case was tried in the late 1960s, it was until then the largest income-tax refund sought on behalf of an individual ever brought to trial in the federal district court for the Northern District of California.

The government had assigned high current values to Georgina's stock and taken millions in taxes. As to the high current values, we had little basis for dispute. By the 1960s, the stock was publicly traded. But our tax claim was based on the difference between what that stock was worth in 1912 and what the estate had sold it for in 1961. From the government's expert appraisers came their opinion that in 1912 the stock of the company then owned solely by Georgina's father was nearly worthless; thus, the entire sales proceeds would be taxable. The IRS approached the taxation process with a vengeance that caused me to detect a resentment on their part that, at the time of Edwina's parents' gifts, there was no law taxing gifts or inheritances. From the IRS perspective, that was truly a lawless and unspeakable state of affairs. They were prepared to remedy it in 1964 by visiting on Mrs. Cole's estate the taxes her parents had not paid, and then some. And they had the experts to do it. It was our job on behalf of the late Georgina Cole to prove that at the time Georgina's parent had given her the stock, the company was already worth a great deal.

The critical challenge for the lawyer in such an instance is to find someone who knows about the matter at issue, and who has the qualifications to testify in court. In addition, it is necessary that such a person be willing to testify, and preferable that he or she can do it well. There are "experts" and experts—the former ready to embrace virtually any subject and talk about it for a fee. The real expert, truly knowledgeable yet willing and able for the forensic fray, is a rarer species. Finding good ones is always a task.

In this case, longevity seemed one reasonable criterion. While some wet-behind-the-ears M.B.A. or Ph.D. economist might have the credentials, I felt that old Judge Wohlenberg would have trouble accepting the current view of a 1912 problem. Another criterion was a long tie to California and the West and a vast knowledge of privately held companies, preferably those holding a lot of physical property—in our case, of course, land and trees.

There is no set procedure in mining for experts, particularly if the area of expertise is unusual. We tried the usual Stanford and Cal business school faculties. No luck. I checked with other lawyer friends and their folklore on experts, with no success. Finally, the venerable Dick Guggenhime, one of my partners, graciously allowed that he knew just the man. Now with a brokerage firm, this person had specialized in private companies and their value throughout his career. He was an expert concerning natural resources and, on top of that, he was an utterly charming fellow.

"The description of an absolute winner of an expert." I exulted.

Dick retorted: "But he has never testified." This did not faze me, nor has it ever done so, for if the expert is genuine the courtroom is the place to prove it. It is the trial lawyer's job to teach the expert how that job is done.

Enter for Georgina the redoubtable Philip Fitzgerald and his sound squire, Dr. Ralph Bing. In visage and demeanor as well as a sense of quest in the courtroom, they were a virtual Don Quixote and Sancho. Phil Fitzgerald, a Dean Witter partner, Boston-educated and seemingly a New England patrician. Old Bay State residents will understand, though, how unlikely to Boston are Irish patricians, and Phil was Irish and Catholic. San Francisco is, however, not Boston and Phil was a patrician here. Tall, gray-haired, with some still discernibly red from a flaming youth, bushy-tailed bright, a smart-appearing person; one who could be an expert in a San Francisco court, even if he was from San Francisco. Phil's prepossessing manner was a product of his combined wit and articulateness. One wanted him to talk on any topic, delivering a monologue that seemed to be a conversation, to present a picture or to create a dream. Fact and fancy might be intertwined; but, as he spoke, they became real.

I checked up on Phil through the usual lawyer scouting channels. Who was old enough to testify credibly about 1912

corporate values? Who knew about natural-resource companies and timber? Who had a feel for old San Franciscans'
sensibilities? Who could powerfully express this in court? The
answer, time and again, was Philip Fitzgerald, Esq. A meeting was arranged.

The Pacific Union Club sits atop Nob Hill in San Francisco.
It was the mansion home of Charles Flood. On the heights
of the hill, California's early entrepreneurial barons—Crocker,
Stanford, Flood, and Huntington—had prowled. Phil Fitzgerald had left Boston for San Francisco fifty years before to
attend the Stanford Business School. He picked up the view
as an undergraduate at Harvard "that if it was worthwhile
for Californians to come east to Harvard to learn, then it
would be worthwhile for an easterner to go west to California
to learn." He did, and, like so many others, decided that
California was the place for him to settle. Employment op-
portunities were good in the heyday of the 1920s, and with
an investment firm here he started as a specialist in West
Coast business. Phil, as only a first generation achiever can,
enjoyed the fruits of his own investment endeavors. Through
his work, he had developed a knowledge and sense of San
Francisco's business past.

Sitting in the walnut elegance of the Pacific Union Club
dining room, liveried waiters at hand, Phil, with the golden
glow of a luncheon martini warming him, interrupted himself
to listen as I explained my unusual needs: "A man, an expert,
wise about old California business, knowledgeable about the
minds of its entrepreneurs in the early twentieth century. A
man, adversary to the United States government and, particularly, the Internal Revenue Service. And, surprisingly, in
this case this person's expertise would call for his testifying
that a business—a company—was worth far *more* than the
government posited, for this would reduce inheritance taxes."

Phil was silent for perhaps three minutes as I defined the
expertise I sought, then vociferously declared himself ready

and able; he reported to enter the lists. "I am your expert, young man. I can do it and I—we—will win. My condition—"

"Yes, Mr. Fitzgerald?"

"—I will count on you to get the family facts to assist me, and I'll do my own prowling, *but* you must also retain my assistant, Dr. Ralph Bing." Enter Sancho.

Dr. Bing was as unlike Philip Fitzgerald, Esq., as are opera stars and country-western singers. Dr. Bing had earned a Ph.D. in Europe and, like many other German Jews, had been forced to emigrate in the 1930s. Using the resources he could take with him, he was able for a year to hone his acute mind further in an American university. As Fitzgerald had done two decades before, he chose Stanford. Bing was an economist by training, by instinct, by design, and by desire.

It was the Stanford connection that produced the initial contact between Bing and Fitzgerald. Even in the 1930s Fitzgerald prospered. Dr. Bing got his first American job as an assistant to Phil. By the 1960s, Phil and Ralph had worked together for three decades, Ralph providing Phil with the economic insight and the facts to analyze investments and to find the good ones. Phil, in turn, knew who might find them attractive, and he had the charm to sell them. The ingenuity of their combined talents had served them both well. Mr. Fitzgerald, better financed from the outset, had invested substantially in what Dr. Bing recommended, and by Dr. Bing's light had become rich. Dr. Bing, who was more conservative and less sure that life always got better, had done well. He was that sort of soul who was not concerned about getting rich, for riches would have produced great worries that he might lose his fortune. On the other hand, he delighted in Fitzgerald's success. While Bing seemed to stand in the tall shadow of the elegant Philip Fitzgerald, both knew and respected one another well, for the reason that Dr. Bing had helped to create the Fitzgerald stature.

As different as they were in temperament, they were even more so in appearance. Dr. Bing was quiet, small, almost

As unlike as opera stars and country-western singers

shabby in appearance. When he talked, his accent-shaped words always portrayed something substantive. He was ever pleased to slip into the shadow of Phil Fitzgerald, which he had helped to create. Bing would be hard to find in a crowd.

What Dr. Bing did like was to make Phil Fitzgerald seem the wisest of investment advisers. He ferreted facts, arranged them with insight, mobilized them with force and logic, and took them to Phil. Phil knew to listen respectfully to Dr. Ralph Bing's ratiocination, absorbing every nuance of Bing's discourse. And from Phil's lips, Bing's vibrant insights came alive and became, in fact, the "truth." When Dr. Bing heard of the new joint mission—to take on the United States government to seek the refund of taxes—he was as excitedly breathless as Phil had been loquacious. We had our experts.

Phil Fitzgerald, while expert in many matters, had never testified in court. Ralph Bing's one day in court had occurred at his naturalization proceeding some twenty years before. Neither was daunted. It was a question of my office's providing facts and documents and Dr. Bing's developing the economic data to support our position. Given this ammunition, Phil would explain the great 1912 wealth of the Wilburs to the court, just as he would make an investment presentation to a group of securities analysts.

Phil instinctively understood the part of the forensic expert. "All I have to do," said Phil, "is to tell the Wilbur story so the judge will be convinced what a fine company it was in 1912, and how well it was managed then, all to show its great value then."

Unfortunately, we would not have a jury. Some conservative tax lawyer had decided the year before I became involved that this "complex" case would best be tried to a judge. Fitzgerald, Esq., was sanguine that, judge or no, he could sell Wilbur Lumber Company Stock, 1912 values, at a very high price.

As a closely held stock, there were, of course, no market prices to look to. Its 1912 value was best established through its underlying assets. Some of the assets had been valued in the 1920s when a member of the Wilbur family had died. We knew, but had little hope for using, IRS values developed in the 1920s inheritance tax proceedings. Phil was piqued at that, for he viewed Uncle Sam's position then as an early shot at redistributing accumulated wealth. "The only thing consistent about the IRS," Bing reported, "is that they'll use the value that will get the greatest tax."

Samoa is not generally recognized as having a California locale. But it does, and, indeed, Samoa, a town in the north of California had long been the headquarters of Wilbur Lumber Company. Dr. Bing and I arranged to travel there to unearth what we could of Wilbur Lumber records, now in the possession of a successor corporation. Philip Fitzgerald, Esq., would do his research in the more comfortable environs of his San Francisco clubs.

Turn the clock of "legal progress" from the 1960s to the 1980s, and the entourage to Samoa would have been a very different one. Then, it was the lawyer who would try the case, togged in old khakis and jacket, and one expert, a rumpled, Jewish scholar-economist seeking evidence for use at trial. Today, the quest would be for records—the more, the bigger the case. The litigation search would be led by a senior associate (no partner for such a run)—disgruntled, perhaps, at a dubious discovery assignment—plus maybe two paralegals aspiring to careers as M.B.A.s or engineers, and all the more so after several seasons in the law's minor league paralegaling it. To aid them would be several clerks who would chronicle each piece of paper pursuant to the paralegal's instructions, based on the organizational outline of the senior associate. The associate litigator making this latter-day pilgrimage wouldn't have the foggiest (or, in Samoa, California, the soggiest) idea of what the case for the courtroom would be. He or she would have been in court annually on a motion matter. The object of this search would be endless facts—more usually than any one mind, or any one judge, can absorb. Quantity, be it in papers produced and copied or in hours spent doing it, is what today's law business is about.

With the law's riches comes a certain esprit. The discovery team demonstrates this. All would be smartly garbed. They would be jockeying for position to drive the large rented vehicles while bemoaning that outpost of civilization, which would have only irregular (semiweekly) and erratic (local-weather-controlled) air service, prohibiting a first-class flight in). Their concerns for the days ahead: Would the motels be livable? What sort of decent restaurants could they find in such an area?

In 1963, it was different. Ralph had opted for riding in my secondhand red Volvo. For me, mileage was desirable for the expense-reimbursement income. Ralph had no enthusiasm for driving. His daily commuting drive from Marin presented enough terror for him. He had the scholar's inability to keep his mind on the road, since there were too many other interesting things to think of. For this, we were later to be indebted.

Highway 101 North was an adventure trail out of San Francisco. It was and is a path into a world as different from the city sophistication of San Francisco as a bonsai tree is from a redwood. Once breaking north of rural Santa Rosa, the hills start a gentle climb into the Land of the Redwoods. The two-lane, winding road was largely unvehicled. The few population centers clustered around bars. At these hamlets stopped loggers and thirsty salesmen heading north to Eureka, Portland, and Seattle, beyond which there was no more.

The Volvo, stick-shift-tenacious of curve and hill, was just the steed with which to face and avoid behemoth lumber trucks hell-bent for random sawmills. The mills were marked by stumpy open furnaces in which sawdust and waste wood burned. By day, they looked like ancient metal creatures belching smoke and steam; at night they glowed, sawdust fire red-spewing. Their flames sparked into the black-blue night sky as if they aspired to join constellations millions of miles above them.

The Promised Land

It was a land marked by its own excesses: sheer size, reckless roads, and an abandoned last use of trees that had been there forever. The lumber mills, wasting their crops prodigiously, devoured trees at the corrugated mill furnaces that resembled launchpads designed by the Wright Brothers. These mills stood as sentinel outposts to the decades of the 1970s and '80s when, for the first time, people would realize that the end of these forests, these clear streams, and the sure, free air were directly in sight.

It was a fitting landscape to provoke the mind of Dr. Bing, scholar squire to Philip Fitzgerald, into reflecting on how A. G. Wilbur, lumber baron of a half-century past, must have regarded his domain and, more importantly, how he would have gone about recording its values.

"*If* they kept records? But of course they kept records," said Dr. Bing. "The question is, did they keep the records A. G. Wilbur kept for fifty years? If these records still exist, then there will be maps; and they may reveal the visions of A. G. Wilbur. And if there are company records, we must hope also to find the personal records of Mr. Wilbur. They will be the key to what the company was worth. Unfortunately, Midas does not keep his gold on public display. We will have hard looking to do."

The ride brought us into contact with a fellow traveler of Highway 101 North, a somewhat errant knight of this road, Mr. Sam "Lucky Lager" MacDonald, unrivaled beer purveyor. We first noted Mr. MacDonald guzzling a breakfast beer with a local barroom owner. We asked them about suitable stops on the road ahead.

"Stop at the Lucky signs all the way to Eureka," Mr. Mac advised. "Those are the places you can trust."

It would have been hard to dispute Mr. Mac's endorsement, for there were few establishments purveying liquor on 101 that were not under Mr. Mac's Lucky sign.

Of growing amazement to Dr. Bing and myself was Mr. Mac's capacity for his own product and survival. At each

Lucky sign, Mr. Mac would stop to renew friendships, get his beer order, quaff a few with the owner, buy a round for the locals, then be off, hell-bent and beer-fueled, for his next stop. Dr. Bing and I proceeded at a slower pace, evenly spreading our conversation through a pleasant day's drive while Mr. Mac bunched his at Lucky bars. We became concerned for his safety and for our own as his big old Cadillac overtook us time and again, as Mr. Mac's brew flowed north.

By day's end in Eureka, we had encamped, this time at the Eureka Inn, a venerable establishment. Mr. Mac, his day's work behind him, was enjoying bourbon at the bar and was delighted to visit again. We were by now quite congenial acquaintances. We told him a little of what we sought.

"Records of a corporation, at least fifty or sixty years old, might be somewhere," Sam allowed. (After hours the honorific "Mr. Mac" was retired.) "People don't throw many things away, and particularly papers. Since many of the working folks up here can't read, they think writing has to be valuable. There is another thing too. Since Wilbur was taken over by Western American, it's got a new building and new people; but I doubt they have the Wilbur records mixed with Western's. Business people keep their own records, and private. My successor won't mine the same veins I do. I just hide my own stuff away in the attic. Someday the grandkids might want to know about what old Sam MacDonald did."

Sam had been working the Eureka environs since World War II. He knew all its bartenders—and because few know more about a community than its bartenders, we pursued with Sam where records might be and who would know about them. One clue he gave us was that "today the Western facility is linked to the world by road travel, but in A. G. Wilbur's glory days, it was all railroad. A. G. Wilbur would come up in his own railroad car, bedroom, office, and all. The tracks where he would have parked and the present Western offices are far apart. Records don't move much. Look in the buildings around the old railroad siding."

Praise be to Sam, for Western with its modern facilities offered nothing. While we had a letter of introduction, courtesy of the bank executor of Georgina Wilbur Cole's will, it served us best by preventing our being completely ignored. The head of the office there, one Clarence Belgium, C.P.A., had a singular distrust for law and lawyers. He was particularly skeptical of lawsuits in which the IRS was a party. While he had been "urged to cooperate," we had the feeling that he felt cooperating with us would be viewed by the IRS personnel evaluating his profits and losses as akin to trading with the enemy.

Within the Western facilities, according to Belgium, there were no Wilbur records. They could not exist because of Western's record-destruction policy, which he personally administered. "Clean out most things every six years or after an audit closes . . . mandatory, all things are gone in 12 years . . . and, so, things from fifty years past just don't exist."

A document-discovery litigator who would not have to face the courtroom might report this, turn back for the Eureka Inn and a hot meal after such hard work, anticipating a return to the amenities of San Francisco while bemoaning the lack of a private railroad car of Wilbur's era to take him home.

Instead, we inquired about the location of the old railroad siding, whether there were still buildings there, and if we might look around. "Quisling" to the IRS or not, Mr. Belgium had to say yes.

Why Samoa, California, was so named is a mystery to me. It was a cold, dank, and flat place on a sort of isthmus—and wet, wet, wet. Perhaps the rain had, on a warm day, stirred vestiges of travel memories in some geographer of early times, or perchance it was viewed as being as isolated as Samoa to some romantic, if misguided, early traveler.

But Samoa it was, and at the shut-down siding of an old railroad we found a long, low, wooden building that looked for all the world like a dockside warehouse. On its sides, faintly appearing, one could see "Wilbur Lumber Company."

Through old but weather-cleaned windows we could observe nondescript piles of boxes and some closed-off rooms.

Back to Mr. Belgium we hied with a request that we be allowed to explore this warehouse he knew nothing of and cared less about. He provided us with a guide, a limping ex-logger, pastured now as a company handyman since his disablement in a logging accident decades past. John Foretell, part Indian, 100 percent logger, hung on in Samoa, as a Wilbur legacy to Western American. A. G. Wilbur himself had promised the young logger when he became disabled that he'd always have a job with the Wilbur company. John Foretell, unaware of vested rights or successor corporations, still appreciated that. It was as if from his grave, A. G. Wilbur ruled and in doing so remained as good as his word to the logger injured forty years ago while in his prime. John Foretell still had his job. He would, for reasons unfathomable to him, even get a pension.

John was an obvious ally and as enthusiastic at the opportunity to aid the dead hand of A. G. Wilbur in enriching his heirs as he was at taking on the government. He had the sound, wise, and justifiable Indian distrust of anything involving the government. We told him that to beat the IRS we had to prove that the Wilbur Lumber Company was worth a great deal in 1912. This made sense to John; if it was worth a lot then, it would still be worth a lot, the nuances of capital gains taxes notwithstanding. As Bing observed, "John's logic is better and more consistent than that of the IRS."

While Foretell was optimistic from the outset, Dr. Bing and I, once inside the musty, dank warehouse, were dismayed. If we had invaded with a litigation attack squad of the eighties staffed by paralegals and clerks, the charge would be to count, index, cross-index, microfilm, and otherwise process the musty boxes of records. We would have replicated, perhaps not once but several times, every A. G. Wilbur Lumber Company time slip, timber-cut record, and shipping order from the beginning of time, all to be assembled in orderly and arbitrary sequence. There would be enough document production to enrich lawyers' coffers for months and enough paper to denude one of A. G. Wilbur's treasured forests. Dr. Bing and I had neither the inclination nor the time and resources for such a production-line attack.

We snooped and sampled a few boxes here and a few more there. We were able to verify some hazy datelines from the cartoned innards of the once proud company. Some records seemed worth scrutinizing—early corporate minutes, circa 1911. These indicated A. G. Wilbur's interest in acquiring more and more land and in not cutting too much timber. There were also timber sales records and stumpage prices, raw data for values. Countless maps were scurried out by John, but there was no lodestar find. We were not shut out, but had no real hits. As the dank day in that wet, ill-lit warehouse closed down, John asked, "What about A. G.'s office?"

"What about it, John?" inquired Dr. Bing.

"It's there. There in the walled-off corner behind that row of boxes."

Indeed, faintly visible at the edge of a circle of light created by the enameled metal lampshade hanging from a single ancient, attenuated wire was a door with three brass letters on it. A closer view made visible the initials A.G.W., desecrated by decades of dust. Gaining entry to the office was no problem. Whatever his logger's disability, it didn't at all affect John Foretell's ability to open the founder's office.

Once inside, it became plain that A. G. Wilbur was a man who made his visions known. Family pictures of his children, small to large, adorned the walls. They walked, they bicycled, they rode horses. A. G. was demonstrably a father concerned for his children's growth and future. The pictures also reflected settings—city, home, country house, forest—and on them were occasional inscriptions. On his son's graduation picture: "John, may Your degree move You to work with me." And of Edwina in a forest setting: "May You Treasure this place forever." The mind's image from the photos showed Mr. Wilbur's boundless esteem for his family and his estate. His words and the pictures bespoke his view of the value of his holdings.

Centered in the room was an ancient rolltop desk, made not of California redwood but of New England oak now rooted in Samoa, California. Again, John Foretell, displaying willingness to do his part for the deceased A. G. Wilbur, had the desk and its drawers open and available for scrutiny. From his pocket he produced a flashlight to aid our search. This time there were maps, not just of Wilbur holdings but of Wilbur aspirations, with areas marked, "Try to Get!", "Worth twice today's price!", and a surprisingly current, "Go for It!" In the far left bottom drawer were more pictures, old letters, and a leather bound "Personal Diary A.G.W." We had found the mother lode.

Dr. Bing's perusal of A. G.'s cryptic notes so brightened him that the dusk of the approaching evening seemed delayed by his intensity. "It's here—how he thought—what he knew—and how much it's worth! With this information, Phil—Mr. Fitzgerald could determine how much value the Wilbur Lumber Company had. I could give him the facts, the figures, but now we have the reasons, the sense of the owner. You will not believe what Mr. Fitzgerald can do with such stuff." The good Sancho had found the stone with which to sharpen his master's rapier tongue.

The ride back was, in every sense, downhill. We had found more than we had hoped. Phil Fitzgerald could take the stand emboldened by Dr. Bing's economics, but also infused with the person of A. G. Wilbur, his family, their future and Mr. Wilbur's 1912 visions and values.

Upon our return to San Francisco, Fitzgerald evinced delight at our report. His own, more comfortable explorations concerning A. G. had been productive. Aged lumber merchants and former bank cashiers now senioritized to bank vice presidencies recalled Wilbur's ways: "He always wanted to accumulate. . . ." "He was ever ready to borrow against what he had to buy more of. . . ." "His ideas about the value of his holdings exceeded good sense."

And campmates from his Bohemia Camp, "The Wayside Log," some of them old enough almost to prove there is life after death, shared intimacies with young (in his late seventies) Phil Fitzgerald: "A. G. loved timberland. He believed it would always be worth more because there was only so much. Why, he forced the club to buy more, at prodigious prices, in the early 1900s to protect our Grove." These purchase records were available and, in Dr. Bing's expert opinion, which became Phil Fitzgerald's, provided good comparable indications of value for Wilbur's other holdings.

This was a case where our evidence seemed to grow much as had A. G.'s redwoods. In pursuit of the potentially mammoth tax refund, I became concerned and conservative. The trial was several months off. Neither side had deposed experts. At the time, either it wasn't the fashion or there was some legal prohibition denying access to the other side's property right in expert knowledge. Not deposing the government expert did not trouble me. We would have the trial testimony transcribed daily. I could study it overnight. The judge would not shorten my cross-examination time, and I was developing the view that the best cross-examination is a one-time courtroom encounter, pitting expert and advocate, without prior deposition testing, in a first-blood struggle of wits and wisdom.

My expert, the distinguished Philip Fitzgerald, Esq., was another matter. He had never testified in court. That, in itself, fazed Phil not a whit, and it did not trouble me unduly. But Fitzgerald might die, and with his passing our chances to get millions for the Georgina Wilbur Cole estate would be lessened. Phil literally had the ability to take Georgina's money to his grave. No lawyer could countenance such an injustice.

Cajoling Mr. Fitzgerald with the notion that a pretrial walkthrough examination would be a great thing for our side, I got him to agree to be deposed *by me.* A mere technicality, I assured him. To do this required a court order to the effect that "Philip Fitzgerald's testimony had to be perpetuated because he was an indispensable witness who might die before trial." Deposing my own expert with the other side present was a livelier type of pretrial exercise than today's private video practice sessions with experts. The government lawyer sensed something was amiss with this unusual request but felt the IRS had much to gain by learning of our very lively witness's "deathbed" opinion in advance. The procedure to perpetuate Phil's testimony was agreed to.

Fitzgerald's deposition went well enough. Under precise, planned questions, Phil told of A. G. Wilbur, his holdings, his family, and of the land's great value. He was nervous. We all were, but Phil warmed to the task. The direct took a solid day. The government lawyer was patient, though frustrated by so long a time listening, and galvanized by what he considered Mr. Fitzgerald's outrageous (to him) answers about value. "A. G. thought the land was priceless, and time has shown him almost right. He wanted to accumulate wealth; and if selling land was the way to do it, he would have. But he kept buying at higher prices."

"Comparables?" The government lawyer inquired. And, in volleying reply: "Of course, what A. G. paid and what he recommended his club pay for redwood acreage; but that value alone was more than three times what the IRS wants to pretend it's worth now so they can tax it."

Mr. Fitzgerald's demeanor, described by a friend as "one that does not suffer fools lightly," ignited the assistant United States attorney to cross examine . . . and cross examine . . . and cross examine. We endured another full day in deposition, a cross-examination longer than my direct—always an indication that one's witness has done well.

The cross ebbed and flowed. The government lawyer was well prepared and had his good moments. I had admonished Phil to hold back, to bide his time for another day. Despite this, at times with frustrating candor, Phil responded at length. Sometimes, drawing on his Irish guile and a lifetime of calculated loquaciousness, he was evasive and confusing in response, yielding few facts—lots of words, but not much information.

Ired by the old gentleman, the government lawyer more and more fired his best shots. He was, I came to realize, wasting a fine cross-examination in a deposition at his client's expense and for my expert's edification. While this adversary-expert encounter was but a preliminary to the trial event, its outcome was bound to scar one of the participants. Phil Fitzgerald was not the one.

Faster than the demise of Phil Fitzgerald came the trial date. Phil Fitzgerald, with Dr. Ralph Bing at his side, was primed to defend A. G. Wilbur's estate and his heirs.

Judge Vorenburg had been on the bench a considerable time. He had served in the state court system with dignity; and in his season, honored by Roosevelt or perhaps Truman, he was appointed as a federal district judge. Bright, but no genius, industrious but only enough to do his work competently, he sat at a time when even in the federal district court, cases still "popped up" to adjudge for trial. There was no individual case-to-judge assignment system then, with a judge controlling the case from its very filing. As a consequence, there could be no aggressive judicial management. Judge Vorenburg's style would be to let justice run its true and proper course with all of the evidence to be hung out for his consideration.

We were pleased enough with the judge. I suspect he was as surprised as I that there was no jury involved. Certainly, he favored jurors as fact finders and money givers in that it took the onus off him. After all, his most consistent contacts were with government lawyers and collegial judges who, like himself, were ultimately compensated from taxes paid to his employer, the United States government. This seldom makes one prone to largess.

The trial proceeded predictably. There were few disagreements about the business of establishing corporate entities, shareholder owners (all Wilburs), and what resources the company had owned in the early 1900s.

We had jollied the proceeding up with some large maps and even current aerial photos of the holdings. One demonstrative-evidence highlight came as the associate working with me was asked to produce for the judge a case on some legal point. Delighted by this opportunity to participate, my colleague charged to the bench, law book in hand, banging into a large map on a stanchion. His bulk knocked the map and a series of pictures to the courtroom floor.

The judge: "Mr. Lundquist, your associate is crashing your case."

Mr. Lundquist: "Your Honor, he is more noted for his legal scholarship than for his presence in the courtroom."

Judge Vorenburg: "Resurrect the shambles and proceed."

I quickly inducted Mr. Fitzgerald as an expert. I asked of his qualifications to testify here. "Examining the free enterprise system since before the twenties," he said, "and counseling wealthy investors and poor widows all my life."

"Military service?"

"Of course. Word War I and some advisory officership post in World War II. I was turned down as a 'little too old' for combat, though I was ready."

Damn! How I missed a jury.

Government counsel offered to stipulate to his expertise; I politely declined.

As an expert witness, Mr. Fitzgerald was all that we had hoped for and more. Dr. Bing's economic acumen had been inhaled and came forth in an opinion delivered with a voice that forced you to listen. His words painted. Everything could have been perceived by a twelve-year-old, and all was clear to the Judge. As fine testimony does, it exceeded the understandable and became interesting. Fitzgerald's economic analysis of trees and forests yielding lumber and homes represented the timber industry as the underpinning of American enterprise for the first half of the twentieth century and beyond. The growth, development, and prosperity of California had, as Fitzgerald told it, "a direct and overpowering link to A. G. Wilbur's wealth and wisdom."

As with most good Irish raconteurs, it was about people that Phil Fitzgerald spoke best. His explanation of A. G. Wilbur dealt, not only with the man's wisdom, business perspicacity, and wealth, but with his heart and soul.

Finally: "Do you have an opinion as to the value of each share of Wilbur common stock in 1912?"

"I do."

"What was it?"

"Nearly priceless, but conservatively $256 a share, then."

"And on what do you base your opinion?"

Now Fitzgerald became lyric. There was, of course, the basic economics, but it was close knowledge of Mr. Wilbur, his family, and his interests that fortified the solid opinion.

While Fitzgerald had listened to and pored over Dr. Bing's economics, he had further synthesized by his own scrutiny, the diary, the family letters, and the trove of pictures. He knew every family member, how they looked at what age, where they had traveled, and the great aspirations Mr. Wilbur had for them. These facts were augmented with anecdotal information from his club brothers. A. G. Wilbur was resurrected in the courtroom.

"See there, he wore a long overcoat for the wet days in Samoa. . . . That's him in the striped jersey and knee-length bathing trousers at the Del Coronado in San Diego where he and Georgina enjoyed her eleventh birthday together. . . . Look, here he is around the campfire with his Bohemian campmates joining in song and sociability." Fitzgerald's words created a benevolent, loving man, out to make a fortune for his family, and the way to do this was to accumulate timber holdings.

Fitzgerald even recalled (without disclosing that it came from the diary) that A. G. felt he was right to hold onto the company for, in the twenties, the government had valued a very small percentage of stock, transferred by another family member, at $190 a share. "Not enough! A. G. knew full well the value of his large holdings years before."

Once our case was in, I felt serene. The government's cross-examination fizzled. In the lengthy deposition cross-examination, the assistant United States attorney had tipped his hand, and Fitzgerald was ready for anything. Phil Fitzgerald's basic testimony was untouchable.

Very much as an anticlimax, the government's expert witness, a solid, older man, but not old enough to be a peer of Fitzgerald's, took the stand. He was a decent if pedantic, expert giving as good as his government-rate compensation warranted, an economist supplied by Standard & Poor. "Basic facts . . . no demand for timber . . . a recession circa 1912-1914 . . . little value for closely-held companies with restricted income." His opinion as to value then: ". . . between $66 and $76."

The risk I faced in cross-examination was principally that I might improve his direct. Mr. Standard & Poor did have numerous papers and documents with him, including some in his coat pocket. I felt that there was little risk to ask to look at these. He produced them except for the coat-pocket article. I asked, "Could I see that, too?"

Reluctantly: "Yes."

It was, as he had to concede, a very recent Standard & Poor article written by him and criticizing the very theory he employed to value A. G. Wilbur's stock!

The case meandered on as cases do even after they are over. We briefed. The government briefed. We replied. Proposed Findings and Conclusions were prepared, exchanged, objected to. New ones were filed, exchanged, and objected to in that procedural dance that gives lawsuits a life of their own. We all knew the only thing that counted was the per-share figure the judge had jotted down as his value finding at the trial's end.

My associate John Cutler and I had several triumphal lunches at the Pacific Union Club with Phil Fitzgerald and Dr. Bing.

I recall Fitzgerald graciously bestowing on us—"for free,"
though he had been paid well for his Wilbur expertise—
investment advice that, if followed, would have kept me poor
for the rest of my life. "Buy copper." That advice, Dr. Bing
discretely pointed out, was of Phil Fitzgerald's own devising,
not his.

Finally, Judge-in-Due-and-Proper-Course Vorenburg rendered his opinion and value finding: $186 per share! It was
good. Good enough to make the recovery the largest refund
award in northern California to that date. But it was no crop
of gold. The result was well received by our clients. To me
it seemed a fair tribute to litigation professionalism, if not
trial lawyer art.

While we were pleased, we were not elated. Most of all,
we were puzzled. How could the judge have missed our
evidence? How could he give any credibility to the Standard
& Poor expert and ignore in any way Phil Fitzgerald?

The answer eventually emerged. It was several years later.
I was attending a dinner of some legal nature: judges and
lawyers congenial together. My years at the bar had eased
my discomfort in the presence of judges; Judge Vorenburg,
now semiretired, was my dinner companion.

"That Wilbur case, Lundquist. Fascinating one."

"I thought so, Your Honor."

"And Fitzgerald."

"Yes, sir?"

"Great man. Great expert. Probably the finest I've ever
observed."

Well, that assumption was well-founded, but what then?

"We thought so, Your Honor. The very best."

"And the Standard & Poor man was an ass. I gave his
testimony no weight."

Was the old judge bonkers? Was it too much wine? Had
the tides of time washed out part of his legal beach?

"But you didn't take Fitzgerald's value entirely, sir."

"I know, Lundquist. I know. I would have, but his close
ties to the family, his great personal relationship with A. G.

Wilbur, had to bias him. He was too closely held to the bosom of that family. [Fitzgerald was a young boy in Boston in the Wilbur era!] He was so close to them that I had to discount his value somewhat, because he had to be influenced by their personal friendship."

Releford Frank

O ne of today's litigation practice difficulties is that lawyers inhabit skyscrapers. They seldom enter the
courtroom hustings. When they do, it is on behalf
of some corporate behemoth with millions, if not billions, at
stake. The importance of the battle is measured in dollars.
Money is seen as the grist of their legal mill. In its pursuit,
the real grist—people, and a system designed to do them
justice—often is overlooked.

One of the ways around this ivory-tower relationship with
the court system is for the trial lawyer to accept public-
representative appointments. Decades ago, and indeed in
some places today, it was a normal expectation that good
lawyers would be required to tithe their profession by assignments to represent financially needy individuals. That
worthy practice has been largely and, some say, well put to
rest by the use of public defenders. Even so, on occasion,
public defenders run into conflicts. Therefore, in most juris-
dictions, there is a panel of experienced lawyers who accept
appointments to represent indigent, alleged criminals. Thus

came my client Releford Frank. We were selected for each other by the system.

Releford was a spirited, black gentleman who lived in the East Oakland area. His thirty-eight years had seen him in court on a number of occasions. Our meeting was his first involvement with the feds. Releford had in some manner or another been involved in a "sting" in which a postal agent had arranged for Releford to sell him a considerable amount of United States mail. With typical governmental munificence, the furtive agent spent large sums buying mail from Releford. Releford, it seems, had an instinct for knowing what mail might contain checks. So, the mail he sold to the postal agent was worth more than the price of the stamp.

The Frank family was an honorable one in East Oakland, if not blessed with luck. Its members stayed away from hard crimes. There was no violence in Releford's criminal record. He was righteously provoked at those who dealt drugs. Much of his life was spent scrambling to feed family, and in the minority employment market of East Oakland that is a daily struggle.

The Frank family luck was exemplified by his sister Kate. Rather than become a prostitute or deal drugs to support her children, she tried a day of bank-robbing. It's simple stuff: The bank tellers are trained to respond to robbers quicker than you can do an automatic-teller bank-card withdrawal. A simple note to a teller, "Give me your money," produces a stack of marked bills fast. The culprit is on camera. No alarm is sounded, as this would frighten other customers and disturb banking business. The robber leaves with a modest sum.

On the day Kate started and ended that line of work, she and a few friends did four banks. She earned about sixteen hundred dollars. On her way home from work, Kate was assaulted and robbed. She got a concussion and eight years' time; someone else got the money.

My first meeting with Releford took place in the San Francisco County Jail. Releford is loquacious, has great presence, and is ever the salesman. Even the blue jumpsuit and orange socks, which are the jail's uniform, did not demean him.

I was out to get just the facts.

"Releford," I asked, "are you married?"

"No, sir, but I've lived with Caroline since I was twenty-four and we have two children. I do want to get married."

"Wonderful, Releford. Were you married before you lived with Caroline?"

"No, sir, I wasn't."

"By any chance, did you have any offspring before the two by Caroline?"

"Yes, I did. Nine."

"Nine?! *Nine children?!*"

"Yes, Mr. Lundquist."

"And who was the woman involved there?"

"There was nine women," replied Releford.

"Nine?! Nine women for nine children? Before you turned twenty-four?"

Woodley's proud response: "Yes, sir, Mr. Lundquist. Releford Frank don't shoot no blanks."

Unfortunately, the facts in support of Releford's defense offered no revelations that matched his progenital boasts. In fact, after picking at the sting agent, reviewing the government records, and trying to develop some entrapment theory, it was obvious that we had to deal for a plea. This need was particularly acute because Releford had already entered a plea in a state-court criminal matter involving some high-minded commercial fraud—a "Jamaican switch" affair. Releford was adamant that he not get into the state prison system, knowing well that the feds offered better by way of accommodations. With some juggling between the two proceedings, we ultimately arrived at a negotiated plea, with a further state court arrangement that he could serve concurrent federal time for that offense.

The lead in our work for the plea had been undertaken by Mike Shepard. Mike had gone all out, even arranging for Releford and Caroline to be married in court while Releford was in jail. A married defendant is a plus for plea purposes. It was no hurried prison wedding. The children were there, enjoying their parents' being wed at an age when many children are first seeing their parents divorced. Releford was sent to his court wedding in prison garb. Mike, a romantic bachelor, was offended, and he protested. The judge, a kind and wise woman, quickly agreed with Mike that one should not approach the state of holy matrimony in prisoner garb, and she held up the wedding so that Releford could don a civilian suit. Mike provided the flowers and stood in as Releford and Caroline remedied one of Releford's earlier legal oversights. Unfortunately, the honeymoon would have to await completion of Releford's jail time.

The day of the sentencing in federal court at last arrived. Presiding was a visiting federal judge from North Dakota. Mike spoke on behalf of Releford. Representing a criminal about to be sentenced is a delicate matter for a lawyer. I had reminded Mike what a good judge friend told me. The judge always wrote down what he was disposed to sentence before the lawyer began to speak. He tried thereafter never to impose a greater sentence, no matter how long the lawyer talked or how ludicrous the argument. Mike took this to heart; his explanations on Releford's behalf were short and eloquent.

Releford's record turned from dross to gold as Mike spoke. It soon became apparent that this solid North Dakota jurist was not interested in visiting upon this East Oakland entrepreneur a long sentence, particularly in view of the government's substantial involvement in buying mail from Releford. By Mike's telling, if not for enticement by the agent, Releford would probably be making whatever honest living he chose in Oakland. The judge was impressed but he did have a personal curiosity about the pending state court charge for which the state judge had indicated Releford would serve concurrent time. The probation record had reported the Jamaican switch.

The judge said that among the blessings of his visits to San Francisco was enhancement of his general education. Although he thought Mike had explained everything well, he wanted to find out what a Jamaican switch was. Mike replied. Mike's explanation was fulsome, if obscure. One would have thought that the Jamaican switch involved no more than little boys tricking each other in the exchange of toys. The judge seemed satisfied.

Releford, on center stage and not admonished that he shouldn't speak about this particular matter, said, "Your Honor, sir, if I might. Mr. Shepard ain't got it quite right. A Jamaican switch—it's the American way. It's free enterprise. It goes like this: You find someone, someone new in town, who don't know his way around too much. He trusts you. Just like a big corporation sells you something. Like, you let him hold some of your money. He likes you. And then, maybe, he asks you to hold some of his money. And you start holding more of his money than he does of your money. And he trusts you so much that he don't get it all back. Nothing violent. Free enterprise is at work; money is flowing from him to me."

Good-bye, Releford.

Releford has not been daunted by these events. He remains close to his lawyers and calls us *collect* whenever the opportunity affords itself. There's a limitation on the collect calls one can make from prison. In a recent call, Releford was delighted to report that he had been such a good prisoner that he was being granted conjugal visitation rights. Caroline could come to see him and spend the weekend. There was a small problem. He reached me to see if I could solve it. Caroline did not have a credit card, and could not get a rented car because she didn't have a telephone. She did have the money for the rent-a-car, however. If I would just lend her my credit card over the weekend, she could get to see Releford. I would, of course, be paid in advance for the rental car charge to show that Releford could be trusted.

As I explained to Releford, I did want to lend my credit card to Caroline, and certainly would have, but my young partner, Mike Shepard had been so close to them and had been so involved in their family matters, including the wedding, that I knew he'd feel badly if they got to use my credit card instead of Mike's. Therefore, the next time Releford could make a collect call, it should be to Mike to talk to him about it. Releford understood the answer. He has respect for wise counsel.

In Summation

I know trial lawyers who actually get sick when they face a pending trial or when they are constructing a crucial closing argument. It is not atypical for a lawyer, when retained in a case where the opposing counsel is a longtime friend, to call and announce the friendship is suspended until the trial is over. Conversely, within the litigation fraternity I know many lawyers who play out the practice season of motions and discovery and pretrial only to consistently end up settling before the main event. Then there are those attorneys who leave the trial arena altogether because the adversary process exacts too high a price on friendship and health. Life is awfully short.

Why, then, would one aspire to a professional life of sleepless nights and churning stomachs as one "goes in" to address a jury, argue a matter before a judge, or cross-examine an expert? Why do legions of young lawyers seek out a career ultimately measured in wins or losses?

It is tempting to answer this question in grandiose terms, to represent the trial lawyer as larger than life, a professional of mythic proportions. After all, to many, the trial attorney is *the* prototypical lawyer. This powerful, legendary image of the trial advocate achieved its vitality historically. We are direct progeny of those who once resolved disputes through trial by combat. Fortunately for today's lawyers, actual weapons are eschewed. However, just as in battles of old, lives are at stake, issues critical to the public weal are determined, and the very fabric by which society is bound can be woven or torn asunder in the courtroom.

What calls one to this modern-day battlefield? Trial advocacy excites like nothing else does. No two cases are alike, no two judges, no two witnesses, and it is at its core *a people business*. The trial arena is one in which individuals see their lives most intimately bared: Family disputes, divorce, child custody, mental stability, basic economics, welfare problems, personal injuries, crime, and commerce are quotidian courthouse affairs. But the trial attorney's love of the work is not rooted in voyeurism, nor simply in the competitive fact that one side wins, one loses, and you're measured on your record.

The answer to why trial lawyers are ineluctably drawn to this unremittingly challenging profession is deeper than any single lawyer's response. The trial court is the keystone of what makes sense about America. It embodies much of the American dream. David can meet Goliath and win. Injustice and injury pay their price. Rules unfair or unresponsive can be changed. Wealth is not necessary as a key to the courthouse door. What a party has to say about a cause can be said to jurors who will listen and assess. Few who have the chance to speak their piece go away unhappy, even if they do not prevail. Fundamental rights have a forum in which both individual and public concerns are measured—concerns not only for personal gain, but even for the very earth around us, its air, its water.

Some say this trial business is inordinately expensive, a hindrance to progress, the quintessential snafu. But it is, in fact, one of America's most attractive bargains, less expensive by far and more progressive by light years than the follies of most governmental or even business spending. People sense this, and people sense that the lawyers who work at it in our courthouse temples have a special place in working with the values that create our laws. And people accept that values can change if justly considered. The trial lawyer knows this intuitively from clients, from juries, from judges.

The trial is a competition with our past and for our futures. It is competition for change, worked out on the frontiers of societal progress. Federal district courthouses or state trial courts mark that frontier's edge. Frontiers for change are what individuals seek who are motivated by high minds. To work at the limit of the unknowable, as the trial lawyer does, is indeed to have a career of high regard. Small wonder, then, that, each year, young lawyers choose to enter as warriors onto this unique battlefield where ideas and honest intellect are the weapons, justice is the product, and the service rendered is essential to our best values. This is what the law is all about. This is what draws the trial lawyer to the courthouse day after endless day.